Excel
Get the Results You Want

Years 3–4
Opportunity Class Tests
Skills and Strategies

Lyn Baker, Sharon Dalgleish,
Tanya Dalgleish, Donna Gibbs
& John Moir

PASCAL
PRESS

© 2023 Lyn Baker, Sharon Dalgleish, Tanya Dalgleish, Donna Gibbs, John Moir and Pascal Press

Completely new edition incorporating 2021 Opportunity Class test changes

Reprinted 2024

ISBN 978 1 74125 707 6

Pascal Press Pty Ltd
PO Box 250
Glebe NSW 2037
(02) 9198 1748
www.pascalpress.com.au

Publisher: Vivienne Joannou
Project editor: Mark Dixon
Edited by Mark Dixon and Rosemary Peers
Proofread by Mark Dixon
Answers checked by Peter Little and Dale Little
Cover by DiZign Pty Ltd
Typeset by lj Design (Julianne Billington)
Printed by Vivar Printing/Green Giant Press

Contents

Year 3

INTRODUCTION

ABOUT THIS BOOK

The aim of this book is to identify, develop and practise skills and strategies in test situations; in particular, the NSW Opportunity Class Placement Test.

This book will help students organise their thinking—creatively and systematically—when faced with tests, with the object of helping them become more effective and independent thinkers. To this end, thinking strategies suitable for solving the types of questions in the various test areas have been provided.

Note: It must be said that there can be no guarantee of 'carry-over' of a particular skill or strategy from one situation or problem to another. However, there is little doubt that practice can at least make 'closer to perfect' and should certainly lead to a child gaining greater familiarity and confidence which is so advantageous when taking a test. Hopefully, the strategies included will go further than that and provide the basis for the positive thinking so necessary to being successful.

The book is divided into two parts. Part 1 (Year 3) and Part 2 (Year 4) consist of the following:

1 Explanation pages
These include:

- the skill to be practised
- sample questions
- an explanation that relates the skill to the types of test questions
- suggested solutions and strategies.

2 Practice questions
These are follow-up questions to practise the skills covered in the explanation pages.

3 Sample tests
At the end of Year 3 and Year 4, there are sample tests for students to practise based on the NSW Opportunity Class Placement Test.

4 Answer pages with explanations
These include additional suggested methods to help with the student's thinking in answering the questions.

ABOUT THE OPPORTUNITY CLASS TEST

The NSW Opportunity Class Placement Test is required for placement in an Opportunity Class in a NSW public school.

This type of class offers an extra challenge for academically gifted students with high potential in Years 5 and 6. Selection is based on academic merit.

Students are usually in Year 4 when they apply for opportunity class placement and take the test.

Details are available at: https://education.nsw.gov.au/public-schools/selective-high-schools-and-opportunity-classes/year-5.

The tests were updated in 2021 with a greater emphasis on literacy, thinking skills, mathematical reasoning and problem solving. The General Ability Test has been replaced by a Thinking Skills Test. The new NSW Opportunity Class Placement Test adjusts and balances the weighting given to the Reading, Thinking Skills and Mathematical Reasoning components. These changes were in response to the findings of the 2018 Review of Selective Education Access report, commissioned by the NSW Department of Education.

INTRODUCTION

The NSW Opportunity Class Placement Test consists of three multiple-choice tests:

- **Reading** (25 questions in 30 minutes)
- **Thinking Skills** (30 questions in 30 minutes).
- **Mathematical Reasoning** (35 questions in 40 minutes)

About the Reading Test

The NSW Opportunity Class Placement Test includes a reading comprehension component that asks you to read a number of texts and then answer questions to show how well you understood them. The question format for the Opportunity Class Placement Test varies from subsection to subsection. At the time of writing, the question format is as follows for the four subsections:

- Literary prose text—multiple-choice questions on a single text or extract from a text
- Poetry—multiple-choice questions about a poem or extract from a poem
- Factual text—a task which asks you to place sentences or phrases into an information text in a sequence that makes sense (a cloze task)
- Varied short texts—matching descriptive statements to four short texts on the same theme but with different content and written in different styles or from different perspectives.

About the Thinking Skills Test

Thinking skills involve two disciplines: critical thinking and problem solving.

Critical thinking means the ability to analyse a claim or argument, identify whether it is flawed or uses correct reasoning, and determine whether the evidence,

assumptions and conclusion are warranted. Problem solving as a thinking skill means the ability to use numerical or mathematical skills to work out solutions to problems. Critical-thinking and problem-solving skills are valuable in everyday life as well as in many fields of endeavour students might eventually embark upon.

Critical thinking

In order to answer these kinds of questions you firstly need to read and comprehend any information provided and then work out what you need to do to answer each question.

You will need to use a mixture of the following thinking skills:

- identifying the main idea or conclusion in a text
- drawing a conclusion
- eliminating incorrect conclusions
- assessing evidence used to reach a conclusion
- evaluating evidence to strengthen or weaken arguments
- applying reasoning
- detecting mistakes in reasoning.

Before you start, check how many questions there are and the time allowed to complete the test. This will help you work out the average amount of time you should allocate to each question. For example, 30 questions in a 30-minute test means you need to try to answer each question in an average of one minute. If you take longer than two minutes on any one question, you should have a guess and then leave that question and return to it when you have attempted all the questions if you have time left.

You will find some questions faster and easier to complete. Other questions will

INTRODUCTION

require more time to read or may have a twist that you need to consider very carefully.

These questions might have an answer that seems obviously correct at first glance. Be careful: it could be a trap for people who are not using their critical-thinking skills. Don't rush your answers but be aware of your time constraints.

1 Each test question includes a text. This is usually an argument or opinion text. Read the text carefully.

2 Read the question and work out what the question is asking you to do. For example, is it asking you to identify the answer that is correct or incorrect; that is true or cannot be true; that strengthens or weakens an argument; or that shows someone's reasoning is flawed or correct?

3 Read the answer options carefully and work out which answer you think is correct.

4 Reread the text and the question to make sure you have worked out the correct answer. Be mindful of the time.

5 When you have finished, use any leftover time to check your answers.

Problem solving

These types of questions could be thought of as puzzles to solve, rather than problems. Like other puzzles they can be fun to work out and you can get a real sense of satisfaction from finding the correct answer.

As with other types of questions the most important thing is to read the question carefully. Although time is limited in the test, it is important to take some time to stop and think. With multiple-choice questions the options always include plausible incorrect answer options; if you rush, you might fall into the trap of selecting one of these.

Questions might require solving word problems, placing items in order, finding patterns, manipulating shapes or applying logic. There is no simple rule about how to approach these types of problems. The best possible preparation is to work through lots of practice questions.

About the Mathematical Reasoning Test

Mathematical reasoning involves numbers and patterns, measurement and geometry, and statistics and probability. Questions might be given in words or may involve a diagram, graph or table. You will be familiar with the topics covered but the questions might be posed in a different way.

Questions involving mathematical reasoning can usually be solved using the same skills commonly used in class. Sometimes you can use trial and error with the options to see which one will give the required result.

Being familiar with the types of questions that might be asked is one way to overcome some of the anxiety and uncertainty associated with tests.

Importantly, don't waste too much time on any one question. If not sure of the answer, leave the question and come back to it later if you have time. Make sure you answer every question—even if you have to guess.

Reading answer sheet

Mark your answers here.

To answer each question, fill in the appropriate circle for your chosen answer.

Use a pencil. If you make a mistake or change your mind, erase and try again.

You can make extra copies of this answer sheet to mark your answers to the two Sample Reading Tests in this book.

1 A B C D ○○○○	6 A B C D ○○○○	11 A B C D E F ○○○○○○	16 A B C D ○○○○
2 A B C D ○○○○	7 A B C D ○○○○	12 A B C D E F ○○○○○○	17 A B C D ○○○○
3 A B C D ○○○○	8 A B C D ○○○○	13 A B C D E F ○○○○○○	18 A B C D ○○○○
4 A B C D ○○○○	9 A B C D ○○○○	14 A B C D E F ○○○○○○	19 A B C D ○○○○
5 A B C D ○○○○	10 A B C D E F ○○○○○○	15 A B C D ○○○○	20 A B C D ○○○○

Thinking Skills answer sheet

Mark your answers here.

To answer each question, fill in the appropriate circle for your chosen answer.

Use a pencil. If you make a mistake or change your mind, rub it out and try again.

You can make extra copies of this answer sheet to mark your answers to all the Sample Thinking Skills Tests in this book.

1 A B C D ○○○○	6 A B C D ○○○○	11 A B C D ○○○○	16 A B C D ○○○○
2 A B C D ○○○○	7 A B C D ○○○○	12 A B C D ○○○○	17 A B C D ○○○○
3 A B C D ○○○○	8 A B C D ○○○○	13 A B C D ○○○○	18 A B C D ○○○○
4 A B C D ○○○○	9 A B C D ○○○○	14 A B C D ○○○○	19 A B C D ○○○○
5 A B C D ○○○○	10 A B C D ○○○○	15 A B C D ○○○○	20 A B C D ○○○○

Mathematical Reasoning answer sheet

Mark your answers here.

To answer each question, fill in the appropriate circle for your chosen answer.

Use a pencil. If you make a mistake or change your mind, erase and try again.

You can make extra copies of this answer sheet to mark your answers to all the Sample Mathematical Reasoning Tests in this book.

1	A B C D E ○○○○○	6	A B C D E ○○○○○	11	A B C D E ○○○○○	16	A B C D E ○○○○○
2	A B C D E ○○○○○	7	A B C D E ○○○○○	12	A B C D E ○○○○○	17	A B C D E ○○○○○
3	A B C D E ○○○○○	8	A B C D E ○○○○○	13	A B C D E ○○○○○	18	A B C D E ○○○○○
4	A B C D E ○○○○○	9	A B C D E ○○○○○	14	A B C D E ○○○○○	19	A B C D E ○○○○○
5	A B C D E ○○○○○	10	A B C D E ○○○○○	15	A B C D E ○○○○○	20	A B C D E ○○○○○

Identifying the meaning of a word in context

ACTIVITY: You need to work out what the context is and how it gives meaning to the word. The context is everything which influences, acts on or is connected with the word in the text.

Read the text below then answer the question.

The teacher's assistant

The teacher's assistant was coming! The entire class burst into activity to conceal their games and look studious. Everyone had a plan: the 'drawing' game desk group pushed their drawings into their laps, the 'plasticine' desk group squeezed the plasticine into their pockets and the 'cards' desk group hid their paper-made cards in their desk drawer. But Sen didn't notice.

The classroom was somewhat crowded, lined with desks arranged into a rigid 7 x 4 grid. It was 2002 in the heart of North-east China and the Year 3 students were currently in their favourite part of the day: study revision. Not that they loved study; rather this was the only time in the day when their class teacher was not there. And the teacher's assistant only checked the class every 20 minutes. There wasn't a single kid in the class who didn't stare at the clock every day waiting for the sacred 2:30 – 4:30 pm period.

Sen put her heart and soul into everything she did. Especially beating her classmates at cards. No-one enjoyed this more than she. Before the teacher entered, she was almost going to win the round. Now the teacher was here and her paper cards were still on the desk!

Sen's deskmate, Shuxuan, elbowed her in the arm. Sen jerked her head up and started sweating. It was too late. The teacher's assistant was already there. Now, if she got rid of the cards the movement would be too obvious. She had to hope the teacher's assistant didn't look over at her desk.

The teacher's assistant cleared her throat. 'Student Sen!'

Sen straightened up and responded promptly, though in a slightly higher-pitched voice than usual.

'Here!'

'Tell your corner to be quiet.'

With that, the teacher's assistant left the classroom. Sen smiled from ear to ear and without a moment's hesitation went back to playing cards with Shuxuan and her corner.

© Harper Cummins; reproduced with permission

Identifying the meaning of a word in context

SAMPLE QUESTION

The word 'sacred' tells us the 2:30 – 4:30 pm period

A has religious importance for the school.

B is highly valued by the students.

C has compulsory attendance.

D makes the students feel as if they are in church.

STRATEGY

Words can change their meanings in different contexts so it is essential to think about the context: where the word occurs and how it fits in.

The word 'sacred' is normally used in a religious context. It describes something that is holy and highly respected by the church community. Here it is used in the context of the school. You need to consider who thinks of the time-slot as 'sacred', what kind of feelings they have towards it and why it matters them.

Now look at options **A–D** and decide which best answers the question.

B is correct. The word 'sacred' is used to show this is the timeslot the students wait for and value most highly. It is a time when they can secretly play games so it is very special to them!

A is incorrect. The timeslot matters to the students, not to the school as a whole.

C is incorrect. Although everyone is expected to attend, this is not the reason the timeslot is described as 'sacred'.

D is incorrect. There is no evidence it makes the students feel as if they are in church.

Interpreting meanings by working out what is implied

ACTIVITY: You need to look for meanings that aren't directly stated in the text. These will be suggested or hinted at by the tone used or from clues that alert you to what is implied.

Read the text below then answer the question.

The teacher's assistant

The teacher's assistant was coming! The entire class burst into activity to conceal their games and look studious. Everyone had a plan: the 'drawing' game desk group pushed their drawings into their laps, the 'plasticine' desk group squeezed the plasticine into their pockets and the 'cards' desk group hid their paper-made cards in their desk drawer. But Sen didn't notice.

The classroom was somewhat crowded, lined with desks arranged into a rigid 7 × 4 grid. It was 2002 in the heart of North-east China and the Year 3 students were currently in their favourite part of the day: study revision. Not that they loved study; rather this was the only time in the day when their class teacher was not there. And the teacher's assistant only checked the class every 20 minutes. There wasn't a single kid in the class who didn't stare at the clock every day waiting for the sacred 2:30 – 4:30 pm period.

Sen put her heart and soul into everything she did. Especially beating her classmates at cards. No-one enjoyed this more than she. Before the teacher entered, she was almost going to win the round. Now the teacher was here and her paper cards were still on the desk!

Sen's deskmate, Shuxuan, elbowed her in the arm. Sen jerked her head up and started sweating. It was too late. The teacher's assistant was already there. Now, if she got rid of the cards the movement would be too obvious. She had to hope the teacher's assistant didn't look over at her desk.

The teacher's assistant cleared her throat. 'Student Sen!'

Sen straightened up and responded promptly, though in a slightly higher-pitched voice than usual.

'Here!'

'Tell your corner to be quiet.'

With that, the teacher's assistant left the classroom. Sen smiled from ear to ear and without a moment's hesitation went back to playing cards with Shuxuan and her corner.

© Harper Cummins; reproduced with permission

Interpreting meanings by working out what is implied

SAMPLE QUESTION

Why does Sen's voice change pitch?

A She has a cold that changes the pitch of her voice.

B She is feeling excited that she might win her card game.

C Shuxuan is tickling her and she is trying not to laugh.

D She is nervous she is about to get into trouble.

STRATEGY

You need to read between the lines of the text to find what is hinted at or suggested but not directly stated.

The story is building to a climax when Sen's voice shifts to a slightly higher pitch. She has already begun to sweat, which is a clue that she is feeling anxious. You can work out she thinks the teacher's assistant is about to punish her for playing cards instead of studying. How would she be feeling?

Now look at options **A–D** and decide which best answers the question.

D is correct. When the teacher's assistant speaks to Sen, she realises she has not hidden her cards as the other students have done. Her nervousness that she might be about to get into trouble makes her voice go higher in pitch.

A and C are incorrect. There is no mention of Sen having a cold or of Shuxuan tickling her.

B is incorrect. She has stopped playing cards when the teacher's assistant speaks to her.

PRACTICE QUESTIONS

Read the text below then answer the questions.

The teacher's assistant

The teacher's assistant was coming! The entire class burst into activity to conceal their games and look studious. Everyone had a plan: the 'drawing' game desk group pushed their drawings into their laps, the 'plasticine' desk group squeezed the plasticine into their pockets and the 'cards' desk group hid their paper-made cards in their desk drawer. But Sen didn't notice.

The classroom was somewhat crowded, lined with desks arranged into a rigid 7 x 4 grid. It was 2002 in the heart of North-east China and the Year 3 students were currently in their favourite part of the day: study revision. Not that they loved study; rather this was the only time in the day when their class teacher was not there. And the teacher's assistant only checked the class every 20 minutes. There wasn't a single kid in the class who didn't stare at the clock every day waiting for the sacred 2:30 – 4:30 pm period.

Sen put her heart and soul into everything she did. Especially beating her classmates at cards. No-one enjoyed this more than she. Before the teacher entered, she was almost going to win the round. Now the teacher was here and her paper cards were still on the desk!

Sen's deskmate, Shuxuan, elbowed her in the arm. Sen jerked her head up and started sweating. It was too late. The teacher's assistant was already there. Now, if she got rid of the cards the movement would be too obvious. She had to hope the teacher's assistant didn't look over at her desk.

The teacher's assistant cleared her throat. 'Student Sen!'

Sen straightened up and responded promptly, though in a slightly higher-pitched voice than usual.

'Here!'

'Tell your corner to be quiet.'

With that, the teacher's assistant left the classroom. Sen smiled from ear to ear and without a moment's hesitation went back to playing cards with Shuxuan and her corner.

© Harper Cummins; reproduced with permission

1 What does the phrase 'the "plasticine" desk group' mean?

  A the group using a desk made of plasticine

  B the group made of plasticine

  C the group playing with plasticine to do their school work

  D the group playing with plasticine to avoid studying

2 Shuxuan elbows Sen in the arm because

  A she wants to make Sen laugh.

  B she is clumsy.

  C she is warning her of the teacher's assistant's arrival.

  D she wants the teacher's assistant to notice Sen.

☞ Answers and explanations on page 110

Making a judgement about a character

ACTIVITY: You need to consider all the information you are given about the character: their words and actions, their relationships, and what others think or feel about them. You must think critically about this information to make a judgement.

Read the poem below by Donna Gibbs then answer the question.

Who am I?

Who am I?
My body is unusual—
without a bone or limb.
I have no teeth. I have no eyes.
I'm both a her and him!

You might think me a baldy.
In fact, you would be wrong.
There are hairs on all my segments and
I'm muscly, slim and strong.

Anterior to posterior
I'm a very handsome chap.
Cut off my tail, I'll not complain.
I rarely fuss or flap.

I'll simply grow a new tail,
get on quickly with my work.
I'll shift the soil. I'll help it breathe,
recycle all your murk.

The truth is I'm a hero
so why do people squirm?
It's time I got a medal.
I'm a prize-deserving worm!

© Donna Gibbs; reproduced with permission

SAMPLE QUESTION

How trustworthy is the worm as a narrator?

A not at all: he is boastful and makes everything up

B not very: about half of what he says is exaggeration

C quite: some of what he says is accurate

D very: almost everything he says is accurate

STRATEGY

You need to make a judgement based on evidence about what the character does and says in the text from your own knowledge about the character.

To make a judgement about the trustworthiness of the worm as a narrator you will need to think about the truth of the claims made. You can draw on what you know to be facts about worms and compare this with what the worm says. What proportion of what he says is true?

Now look at options **A–D** and decide which best answers the question.

D is correct. Although the worm is boastful, his boasts are based on facts. Every detail he gives about himself is accurate except, perhaps, his claim to be 'a handsome chap' and a hero who deserves a medal.

A is incorrect. The worm doesn't make everything up: he states facts about himself.

B is incorrect. Most of what he says is not exaggeration.

C is incorrect. More than some of what he says is accurate.

Identifying the tone used by the speaker

ACTIVITY: You need to critically consider the author's/speaker's language choices and how these convey their attitude or mood (e.g. anger, suspicion, dislike or pride).

Read the poem below by Donna Gibbs then answer the question.

Who am I?

Who am I?
My body is unusual—
without a bone or limb.
I have no teeth. I have no eyes.
I'm both a her and him!

You might think me a baldy.
In fact, you would be wrong.
There are hairs on all my segments and
I'm muscly, slim and strong.

Anterior to posterior
I'm a very handsome chap.
Cut off my tail, I'll not complain.
I rarely fuss or flap.

I'll simply grow a new tail,
get on quickly with my work.
I'll shift the soil. I'll help it breathe,
recycle all your murk.

The truth is I'm a hero
so why do people squirm?
It's time I got a medal.
I'm a prize-deserving worm!

© Donna Gibbs; reproduced with permission

SAMPLE QUESTION

What is the tone of the last two lines?

A   complaining

B   concerned

C   confident

D   anxious

STRATEGY

The tone is the attitude of the speaker to the subject. You need to look at the words used and the values and attitudes they suggest.

The worm boastfully refers to himself twice in these lines. The words he uses are 'medal' and 'prize-deserving'. What does this reveal about his attitude? Does he believe what he is saying and does he speak with assurance?

Now look at options **A–D** and decide which best answers the question.

C is correct. The worm confidently asserts his belief that he is a worthy fellow and deserves to be awarded with a medal for his activities.

A is incorrect. Although he feels badly done by as he makes people 'squirm', in the last two lines he is expressing his confidence that his achievements should be rewarded.

B and D are incorrect. There is no sign of concern or anxiety in his words.

PRACTICE QUESTIONS

Read the poem by Donna Gibbs below then answer the questions.

My hair

I'd like a different hair style.
Some stripes of pink or green.
Or maybe have some dreadlocks,
Or add a sparkly sheen.

My hair's so hard to manage.
It likes to turn and flounce.
If only I could tame it.
Get rid of all its bounce.

Of course I could just grow it
Until it's very long,
Or choose a really short cut.
That way I'd not go wrong.

Dad says I need a Mohawk
that sticks up high and straight.
Mum says No! She loves my hair.
Mmm. Perhaps I'd better wait.

© Donna Gibbs; reproduced by permission

1 How does the narrator sound as she thinks about her hairstyle?

A decisive

B vain

C indecisive

D fearless

2 Dad's comment is most likely being said

A humorously.

B sadly.

C seriously.

D anxiously.

☞ **Answers and explanations on page 110**

Identifying how information and ideas are sequenced

ACTIVITY: Sequencing involves putting ideas and information in a logical order. To work out how sentences are connected to each other within a text you need to consider what goes before and after, and how it fits into the whole text.

SAMPLE QUESTIONS

Read the text below then answer the questions.

Three sentences have been removed from the text. Choose from the sentences (**A–D**) the one which fits each gap (**1–3**). There is one extra sentence which you do not need to use.

The seasons

Have you ever wondered why lots of Christmas cards have scenes with snowmen and falling snow or of cosy log fires with people dressed in warm clothes as they open their presents? You can probably work out that in Australia, Christmas is celebrated in summer whereas in Europe it is celebrated in winter.

When the English settled here in the late 18th century, they brought with them their idea of recognising four seasons. **1** _____ In Australia, at the present time, many people still think about the seasons in this way.

First Nations Australians have their own ways of thinking about the year's calendar. The number of seasons they recognise is dependent on what happens in the local area. **2** _____ Some Aboriginal communities recognise as many as thirteen seasons.

Tim Entwhistle, a botanist, thinks it would be more logical and useful to divide the seasons into five in Australia to reflect patterns of environmental change. In his book called *Sprinter and Sprummer*, he argues that the spring flowering season in Australia really begins in August, the last month of winter. **3** _____ Summer, he says, should be four months long which would give us a shorter autumn and winter.

A	In Kakadu, for example, its traditional owners recognise six different seasons.
B	Why do leaves change their colour in autumn?
C	August and September could be a season of their own named Sprinter.
D	These seasons—spring, summer, autumn and winter—each last for three months of the year.

Identifying how information and ideas are sequenced

STRATEGY

Read the entire passage first so you know what it is about. Then read the missing sentences. Find the first space, numbered 1, and think about the subject of its paragraph. Look closely at the sentences before and after the space and work out the sequence of ideas and information. You need to select the sentence that best connects with these sentences. Repeat this procedure for questions 2 and 3.

You need to select the sentence from **A–D** that best connects with these sentences.

1 **D is correct.** In paragraph two, the author is talking about the number of seasons in a year recognised in Australia. In the previous sentence the author explains how when the English settled in Australia they brought the view that there are four seasons. The missing sentence gives the names of these seasons and the length of each. The sentence that follows states that this is still the view held by many Australian people.

2 **A is correct.** In paragraph three, the author is talking about First Australians' attitudes to the seasons. In the previous sentence the author explains that First Nations peoples tend to see the seasons in relation to their local areas. This sentence gives a specific example of a group of people who recognise six seasons. The sentence that follows refers to the number of seasons recognised by other First Nations peoples.

3 **C is correct.** In paragraph four, the author is talking about Tim Entwhistle's way of thinking about the seasons in Australia. In the previous sentence the author explains that Tim Entwhistle suggests it would be helpful to recognise a fifth season in Australia. This sentence explains when this season takes place and what it could be called. The sentence that follows explains how the other seasons could be altered to make this new addition possible.

The unused sentence is B.

PRACTICE QUESTIONS

Read the text below then answer the questions.

Three sentences have been removed from the text. Choose from the sentences (**A–D**) the one which fits each gap (**1–3**). There is one extra sentence which you do not need to use.

Central Station upgrade

There are 42 new escalators being installed underground as part of an upgrade to Sydney's Central Station. **1** _____ These escalators will make Central Station home to the longest escalators in the Southern Hemisphere.

The upgrade is part of the government's plan to improve public transport in the city. It includes adding an underground pedestrian link. **2** _____ It will connect light-rail passengers with suburban trains, buses and regional services. Once the new metro trains are operating, the pedestrian walk will also link to them.

The engineering involved is highly complex. **3** _____ But government sources are optimistic it will create a world-class resource for commuters.

A	Pedestrian site access during construction is via Platform 12 at Central Station.
B	Nine of these escalators are 45 metres long and weigh more than 26 tonnes.
C	This will be 80 metres long.
D	Building has to be carried out beneath the surface as suburban trains run above.

☞ **Answers and explanations on page 110**

Comparing aspects of texts such as forms, structures, ideas and language use

ACTIVITY: You need to understand what each text is about and how it is written. This will enable you to compare the texts so you can choose the one that best provides the answer to the question.

SAMPLE QUESTIONS

Read the two texts below on the theme of fairytale characters.

For questions **1–3**, choose the option (**A or B**) which you think best answers the question.

Which text ...

includes a cunning fairytale character?

1 _____

is about the physically weakest character?

2 _____

shows good overcoming evil?

3 _____

TEXT A

Meanwhile the wolf ran straight to the grandmother's house and knocked at the door.

'Who is there?'

'Little Red-Cap,' replied the wolf. 'I am bringing cake and wine; open the door.'

'Lift the latch,' called out the grandmother, 'I am too weak, and cannot get up.'

The wolf lifted the latch, the door sprang open, and without saying a word he went straight to the grandmother's bed, and devoured her. Then he put on her clothes, dressed himself in her cap, laid himself in bed and drew the curtains ...

Little Red-Cap called out: 'Good morning,' but received no answer; so she went to the bed and drew back the curtains. There lay her grandmother with her cap pulled far over her face, and looking very strange.

'Oh! grandmother,' she said, 'what big ears you have!'

'The better to hear you with, my child,' was the reply ...

Adapted from the Brothers Grimm Fairytale *Little Red-Cap*

Comparing aspects of texts such as forms, structures, ideas and language use

> **TEXT B**
>
> Now the giant no sooner heard this valiant challenge than he rushed forth to the combat, armed with a huge crowbar of iron. He was a monstrous giant, deformed, with a huge head, bristled like any boar's, with hot, glaring eyes and a mouth equalling a tiger's. At first sight of him, St George gave himself up for lost, not so much for fear, but for hunger and faintness of body. Still, commending himself to the Most High, he also rushed to the combat with such poor arms as he had, and with many a regret for the loss of his magic sword Ascalon. So they fought till noon, when, just as the champion's strength was nigh finished, the giant stumbled on the root of a tree, and St George, taking his chance, ran him through the mid-rib, so that he gasped and died.
>
> From *English Fairy Tales*, retold by Flora Annie Steel

STRATEGY

To find which text offers the answer to a question you need to have a good grasp of what each text is about and how it is written.

TEXT A: There are three fairytale characters in this text. The wolf is shown to deceive people in order to carry out his tricky plans to eat humans. The grandmother is very weak and vulnerable as she is unable to get out of bed. Little Red-Cap, her granddaughter, is kind to her as she is in the habit of bringing her gifts. You can work out that Red Cap is deceived by the wolf and is in imminent danger of being eaten!

TEXT B: There are two fairytale characters in this text. St George is presented as a brave champion who is willing to take up the fight against an enemy even when he fears he hasn't the strength and has lost his magic sword. The other character is a 'monstrous giant', a nasty-sounding creature who uses his brute strength to cause harm and destruction to others.

Now look at the questions and decide which text best answers each one.

1 **A is correct.** The wolf slyly tricks Little Red Cap's grandmother into thinking he is Little Red Cap and making her do what he wants her to do.

   B is incorrect. Neither the monstrous giant nor St George use cunning in their battle against each other.

2 **A is correct.** The grandmother is physically weaker than any of the characters in either text. She hasn't even got enough strength to get out of bed.

   B is incorrect. Although St George is feeling weaker than usual, he is still strong enough to fight a monster.

3 **B is correct.** St George is a valiant champion who honours God. He overcomes the monstrous giant who uses brute strength and an iron crowbar to try to kill him.

   A is incorrect. Although you might predict that when the story ends good will overcome evil, at this stage evil has the upper hand.

Read the two texts below on the theme of fairytale characters.

For questions **1–3**, choose the option (**A** or **B**) which you think best answers the question.

Which text ...

1   ends on a note of tension?   _____

2   includes a deceitful character?   _____

3   describes a lengthy physical battle?   _____

TEXT A

Meanwhile the wolf ran straight to the grandmother's house and knocked at the door.

'Who is there?'

'Little Red-Cap,' replied the wolf. 'I am bringing cake and wine; open the door.'

'Lift the latch,' called out the grandmother, 'I am too weak, and cannot get up.'

The wolf lifted the latch, the door sprang open, and without saying a word he went straight to the grandmother's bed, and devoured her. Then he put on her clothes, dressed himself in her cap, laid himself in bed and drew the curtains ...

Little Red-Cap called out: 'Good morning,' but received no answer; so she went to the bed and drew back the curtains. There lay her grandmother with her cap pulled far over her face, and looking very strange.

'Oh! grandmother,' she said, 'what big ears you have!'

'The better to hear you with, my child,' was the reply ...

Adapted from the Brothers Grimm Fairytale *Little Red-Cap*

TEXT B

Now the giant no sooner heard this valiant challenge than he rushed forth to the combat, armed with a huge crowbar of iron. He was a monstrous giant, deformed, with a huge head, bristled like any boar's, with hot, glaring eyes and a mouth equalling a tiger's. At first sight of him, St George gave himself up for lost, not so much for fear, but for hunger and faintness of body. Still, commending himself to the Most High, he also rushed to the combat with such poor arms as he had, and with many a regret for the loss of his magic sword Ascalon. So they fought till noon, when, just as the champion's strength was nigh finished, the giant stumbled on the root of a tree, and St George, taking his chance, ran him through the mid-rib, so that he gasped and died.

From *English Fairy Tales*, retold by Flora Annie Steel

☞ **Answers and explanations on pages 110–111**

Identifying the main idea

ACTIVITY: You need to identify what the creator of the text wants the reader (or listener) to accept as true. The rest of the text will support this main idea.

SAMPLE QUESTION 1

Jacks is a fun game of skill. To play you only need five small stones or pebbles. You scatter them on the ground then pick one up, toss it in the air and while it's in the air pick up one stone off the ground. Continue to toss one stone in the air and pick up another stone until all the stones are in your hand. In the next round start with two stones in your hand, toss one in the air and pick up two stones at a time. In the third round pick up three stones, and so on. For the last round toss all the stones in the air and try to catch them on the back of your hand, then toss them in the air and try to catch them all in your palm. The more you play, the more you'll improve!

Which statement below is the main idea of the text?

A Jacks is a game you can play with stones.

B In the last round, toss all the stones in the air and try to catch them on the back of your hand, then toss them in the air and try to catch them all in your palm.

C Jacks is a fun game of skill.

D The only equipment needed to play Jacks is five small stones or pebbles.

STRATEGY

1 Read the information in the box.

2 Read the question. Which statement is the main idea?

3 The main idea is what the creator of the text wants you to accept as true. It will usually be somewhere in the text. It's often at the beginning of a text but could also be at the end or anywhere else in the text. The rest of the information in the text will support, add to or give you reason to believe this main idea.

4 Read each answer option in turn and evaluate if it is the main idea. Quickly eliminate any answers that are definitely wrong.

C is correct. This statement is the main idea of the text. It is expressed in the first sentence. The writer of the text wants you to believe that Jacks is a fun game of skill. The rest of the text supports the main idea. It tells what you need to play the game and how to play it.

A is incorrect. This statement is true in the text but the fact that you can play Jacks with stones is not the main idea of the text.

B is incorrect. This statement is instructional as it tells how to play the last round of the game. It is not the main idea of the text.

D is incorrect. This statement is a fact in the text but the fact you need five small stones to play Jacks is not the main idea the creator of the text wants you to accept.

Identifying the main idea

SAMPLE QUESTION 2

Volunteer groups around Australia collect preloved toys that might have gone to landfill at the tip. Volunteers repair the toys if necessary and then donate them to children's charities. There are over a million families in Australia that cannot afford to buy toys at Christmas. Don't throw out toys you are finished with. Donate them to charity so they can be recycled for families in need and also help the planet by reducing waste.

Which statement best expresses the main idea of the text?

A Recycling toys is good for families in need and also good for the planet.

B Preloved toys can find a new loving home.

C Over 25 million toys are thrown out every year.

D Australians spend over one billion dollars on new toys every Christmas.

STRATEGY

1 Read the information in the box.

2 Read the question. It asks you to identify which statement best expresses the main idea of the text. The main idea is what the creator of the text wants you to accept as true. The rest of the text will support that main idea.

3 Evaluate each answer option. Quickly eliminate any answers which are definitely wrong. Choose the answer that best expresses the main idea of the text.

A is correct. The main idea that the creator of the text wants you to accept is that recycling toys is good for families in need and also good for the planet. The rest of the text gives more information to support this main idea.

B is incorrect. This statement might be true but it is not the statement that best expresses the main conclusion about recycling toys by donating them to charities.

C is incorrect. The statement that over 25 million toys are thrown out every year supports the argument to recycle toys but is not the main idea of the text.

D is incorrect. The statement that Australians spend over one billion dollars on new toys every Christmas supports the argument to recycle toys but is not the main idea of the text.

Drawing a conclusion

ACTIVITY: You need to evaluate the evidence presented in an argument. A correct conclusion must be supported by evidence. A conclusion is not possible or cannot be true if the evidence does not support it.

SAMPLE QUESTION 1

When Xavier decided to learn to play the harmonica, his music teacher told him that with regular practice he might be able to play some simple songs within three months but that he had to practise for at least thirty minutes every day to have even a chance of doing that.

If the music teacher is correct, which one of the following must be true?

A Everyone can learn to play simple songs on a harmonica within three months if they practise for thirty minutes a day.

B No-one who practises for less than thirty minutes a day has a chance of playing songs within three months.

C Some people who practise for less than thirty minutes a day will be able to play songs within three months.

D Thirty minutes a day is the most anyone will want to practise the harmonica.

STRATEGY

1 Read the information in the box.

2 Read the question. The question wants you to work out which statement must be true.

3 To answer this question you need to identify whether a conclusion must be true that is not stated in the information provided but can be drawn from this information.

4 Read each statement in turn and evaluate whether it must be true.

5 Quickly eliminate any answers that are definitely wrong.

B is correct. The statement that no-one who practises for less than thirty minutes a day has a chance of playing songs within three months must be true based on the teacher's statement: that to have a chance of playing songs on the harmonica after three months of practice you need to practise for thirty minutes every day.

A is incorrect. It cannot be true that everyone can learn to play simple songs on a harmonica in three months if they practise for thirty minutes a day. There are various reasons why not everyone will be able to achieve this. For example, some people may not have any talent or may take longer than others.

C is incorrect. The teacher's statement says that to have a chance of playing songs on the harmonica after three months of practice you need to practice for thirty minutes every day. Therefore no-one who practises less than that will have a chance of playing songs within three months. This statement cannot be true.

D is incorrect. The statement that thirty minutes a day is the most anyone will want to practise the harmonica cannot be true. Some people might want to practise for longer each day.

Drawing a conclusion

SAMPLE QUESTION 2

Billie, Olive, Sage and Zoe are all reserves for the under-tens swimming team. Billie is fastest reserve. The club will take two reserves to an upcoming swimming carnival. Billie seems to be coming down with a cold so the coach has said that if Billie can't attend the swim meet, then Olive will attend in her place. If Billie does attend, then Sage will go and not Zoe.

If Olive does not attend the swim meet, which of the other three will attend?

A Zoe and Sage only

B Billie only

C Sage only

D Billie and Sage only

STRATEGY

1 Read the information in the box.

2 Read the question. You must work out which children will attend the swimming carnival if Olive does not attend.

3 To answer this question you need to draw a conclusion that is not stated in the text but can be worked out from the information provided.

4 There are four children (Billie, Olive, Sage and Zoe) but only two can attend the swim meet. You can already eliminate Olive and judge that Billie will be one of the children attending as she is the fastest reserve and Olive was only going to be able to attend if Billie could not. Next you need to work out whether Sage or Zoe will attend with Billie. The information tells you that 'If Billie does attend then Sage will go and not Zoe'.

5 Use a process of elimination to work out the answer.

D is correct. You can conclude that because Olive is not going then Billie must be going and if Billie is going then Sage will go and not Zoe. The conclusion is that Billie and Sage will attend the swimming carnival as reserves.

A is incorrect. You are told that Sage or Zoe will attend and not both of them. ('If Billie does attend, then Sage will go and not Zoe.')

B is correct. You are told that the club will take two reserves to an upcoming swimming carnival so the conclusion cannot be Billie only.

C is incorrect. You are told that 'the club will take two reserves to an upcoming swimming carnival' so the conclusion cannot be Sage only.

Assessing the impact of further evidence

ACTIVITY: You need to evaluate a claim or argument and judge whether additional evidence will weaken or strengthen that argument.

SAMPLE QUESTION 1

Andy and Marina are eating fruit. Andy has an apple and Marina has an orange.

Andy: 'Apples are really good for you.'

Marina: 'Oranges are healthier than apples because they contain vitamin C.'

Which one of the statements below, if true, best supports Marina's claim?

A   Apples have more fibre than oranges.

B   Apples contain vitamin C and other important vitamins and minerals.

C   Oranges are harder to eat than apples because you have to peel them.

D   Oranges have more vitamin A than apples.

STRATEGY

1   Read the text.

2   Read the question. You need to identify the statement that best supports Marina's claim.

3   Clarify the claim Marina is making. She claims oranges are healthier than apples and supports this claim by stating that oranges have more vitamin C [than apples].

4   Consider the answer options. Any statement about the health benefits of oranges will support Marina's claim.

5   Judge which answer is correct. Try to quickly eliminate answers which are definitely incorrect or irrelevant to the argument. Check all answer options to ensure you have chosen the correct answer.

D is correct. The statement that oranges have more vitamin A than apples supports Marina's claim with extra information that oranges are healthier for you than apples.

A is incorrect. This statement supports Andy's claim not Marina's claim.

B is incorrect. This statement suggests that apples are healthier than oranges so undermines Marina's claim.

C is incorrect. This statement neither supports nor weakens Marina's claim.

Assessing the impact of further evidence

SAMPLE QUESTION 2

> A teacher said: 'Learning to play a musical instrument at school is as important as learning any other subject.'

Which one of these statements, if true, **weakens** the Year 3 teacher's claim?

A Many parents cannot afford to buy their child a musical instrument.

B Playing a musical instrument uses all parts of the brain simultaneously.

C English is the most important subject at school because it is needed for communication in every other subject.

D Music learning supports learning in other areas, including English.

STRATEGY

1 Read the texts.

2 Read the question. You are asked to identify the statement that **weakens** the teacher's claim.

3 Think about what the teacher is claiming: that learning to play a musical instrument at school is as important as learning any other subject.

4 Consider the answer options. Any statement that contradicts or undermines the teacher's claim will weaken it.

5 Judge which answer weakens the teacher's argument. Try to quickly eliminate answers which are definitely incorrect or irrelevant. Check all answer options to ensure you have chosen the correct answer.

C is correct. The statement that English is the most important subject at school because it is needed for communication in every other subject weakens the argument that learning music is as important as any other subject.

A is incorrect. It might be true that many parents cannot afford to buy their child a musical instrument but this statement is irrelevant to the argument.

B is incorrect. The statement that playing a musical instrument uses all parts of the brain simultaneously strengthens the argument that learning music is important for the brain. However, it doesn't strengthen the argument in the box that learning music is as important as any other school subject.

D is incorrect. The statement that music learning supports learning in other areas, including English, strengthens the argument presented in the box that learning music is as important as learning English.

Checking reasoning to detect errors

ACTIVITY: You need to analyse the reasoning used in an argument or claim. If the reasoning holds up, the claim might be accepted. If the reasoning does not make sense or is flawed, the claim or argument can be rejected.

SAMPLE QUESTION 1

Only students who have completed a satisfactory book review will be allowed to attend the special event after school this afternoon.

Alessia: 'Suri has finished her book review so she will attend.'

Charlie: 'Neo has not completed his book review so he definitely won't be able to attend.'

If the information in the box is true, whose reasoning is correct?

A Alessia only

B Charlie only

C Both Alessia and Charlie

D Neither Alessia nor Charlie

STRATEGY

1 Read the information in the box. You are told that students are only allowed to attend a special event if they have completed a satisfactory book review.

2 Read the question. Whose reasoning is correct?

3 Evaluate the statements made by Alessia and Charlie then compare their statements about Suri and Neo with the information in the box. Decide whose reasoning is correct.

4 When you work out whether Alessia or Charlie (or both) are correct, use a process of elimination to select your answer option.

B is correct. Charlie is correct when he reasons that because Neo has not completed a book review he will not be allowed to attend the event.

A is incorrect. Alessia reasons that because Suri finished her book review she will attend the event. Her reasoning is incorrect. Alessia cannot assert that Suri will attend because she does not know whether Suri's book review is satisfactory nor does she know whether Suri will want to attend or be able to attend for reasons other than her book review.

C is incorrect. You can eliminate this answer because you have worked out that Alessia's reasoning is incorrect.

D is incorrect. You can eliminate this answer because you have worked out that Charlie's reasoning is correct.

Checking reasoning to detect errors

SAMPLE QUESTION 2

Ellery and Yun are at the dog park. Ellery has a book in her hand.

Ellery: 'Margo asked me to keep an eye out for her friend Nicola, who'll be here walking a big brown dog. I have to return this novel to her from Margo who's at the dentist and can't get here.'

Yun: 'There's a lady with a big brown dog. That must be her!'

Which one of the following statements shows the mistake Yun has made?

A Margo might want to keep the book a while longer and not return it yet.

B Margo's friend might not have a big brown dog.

C The lady might not want to carry the book while she's walking her dog in the park.

D Just because there's a lady with a big brown dog doesn't mean she's the lady they are looking for.

STRATEGY

1 Read the information in the box.

2 Read the question. Which statement shows the mistake Yun has made?

3 Evaluate Yun's statement in light of the information. You've been told that Margo's friend will be walking a big brown dog.

4 Judge each answer option. Try to quickly eliminate answers that are obviously incorrect.

5 Check all answer options.

D is correct. Yun has seen a lady with a big brown dog and assumed it must be Margo's friend but it might not be. Yun's reasoning is incorrect because there could be other people in the park with big brown dogs.

A is incorrect. This statement contradicts the information in the box which tells you Margo is returning the book. It is also irrelevant because it isn't the mistake Yun has made.

B is incorrect. This statement contradicts the information in the box. You've been told Margo's friend will be there and she will be walking a big brown dog. The statement is also irrelevant because it isn't the mistake Yun has made.

C is incorrect. This could be true but it isn't the mistake Yun has made so is irrelevant to the question.

PRACTICE QUESTIONS

1

The Daintree rainforest in North Queensland is probably the oldest tropical rainforest in the world. It is home to plants and animals that are not found anywhere else in the world. Some people would like to see parts of the Daintree rainforest sold for people to build homes there but that would be a tragedy. The Daintree rainforest needs to be protected for the future.

Which statement best expresses the main idea in the text?

A The Daintree rainforest needs to be protected for the future.

B The Daintree rainforest in North Queensland is probably the oldest tropical rainforest in the world.

C The Daintree rainforest is home to plants and animals that are not found anywhere else in the world.

D Some people would like to see parts of the Daintree rainforest sold for people to build homes there.

2

Mango, pineapple, banana or kiwi fruit are ingredients used in the 'three-fruit salad' served in a cafe at breakfast time. The cook always uses mango plus two other fruits. The cook told wait staff they might not have mango available at breakfast the next day. He said if there's no mango, he'll use pineapple.

If the cook does not use pineapple tomorrow, which of the other fruits will he use in the three-fruit salad?

A mango only

B kiwi fruit and mango

C mango, banana and kiwi fruit

D pineapple, banana and kiwi fruit

☞ Answers and explanations on page 111

3

Not everything you eat can be eaten by your dog.

Which one of these statements best supports the above argument?

A Dogs can eat most fruits and vegetables.

B Dogs need a balanced diet so they get all the nutrition they need for good heath.

C Chocolate is a human food that is toxic for dogs.

D Dogs love to eat human food.

4

Letitia and Harry are at a public swimming pool. Below is a sign at the pool:

NO GLASS ALLOWED IN POOL AREA

Letitia: 'Dad packed a picnic morning tea with scones and jam. I'm looking forward to it after my swim. The jam is in a glass jar. The sign only shows bottles and glasses so we won't be in the wrong if we have jam in a glass jar.'

Harry: 'Even though there's only a picture of a glass and a bottle, I think the sign means anything made of glass is not allowed so you can't take your jam jar in the pool area.'

If the information in the box is true, whose reasoning is correct?

A Letitia only

B Harry only

C Both Letitia and Harry

D Neither Letitia nor Harry

Working with patterns and codes

ACTIVITY: Finding relationships between a set of numbers or shapes is an important feature of many questions in both mathematical reasoning and thinking skills. It is important to be able to identify key parts of a pattern by, for example, looking for similarities or differences. Once a pattern has been identified it might then need to be applied to further parts of the sequence to find the next term (member of a sequence) or a missing piece of the sequence.

Decoding numbers, letters or symbols into a word is a common form of question. The cross-use of numbers and letters can be a difficult concept at first and clear analysis of the information and question is essential. The words and numbers should be regarded merely as symbols in these questions. Looking for patterns, especially similarities, is the key. It is important to have a general strategy that is as simple as possible.

SAMPLE QUESTION 1

> 2   3   5   **?**   12   17   23

What is the missing number in this sequence?

A 6   **B** 7   **C** 8   **D** 9

STRATEGY

To find the missing term in a number sequence the pattern or rule must first be found. The use of a diagram might make the pattern easier to spot.

$$2\ \ 3\ \ 5\ \ ?\ \ 12\ \ 17\ \ 23$$
$$\backslash\ /\backslash\ /\backslash\ /\backslash\ /\backslash\ /\backslash\ /$$

Pattern: +1 +2 +? +? +5 +6

You must identify how the numbers are changing in their order. The diagram shows you that the difference between the first two numbers in the sequence is 1 and the difference between the next two numbers in the sequence is 2.

Then comes the gap for the question mark, the next difference from 12 to 17 is 5, and from 17 to 23 the difference is 6.

The differences between the numbers seem to be growing by one each time. To test out that theory, insert the numbers that would then fit in the gaps: Following +2 would be +3 then +4. Would they fit in the number sequence? $5 + 3 = 8, 8 + 4 = 12$. They fit the series so the missing number would be 8. **C is correct.**

SAMPLE QUESTION 2

> Suppose the number code 1234 represents the word MATE.

What would be the code for the word TEAM?

A 4321   **B** 4213   **C** 3241   **D** 3421

STRATEGY

With test questions like these, your thinking must involve looking not only for similarities but for a pattern of similarities. Instead of moving your eyes backwards and forwards all the time as you work and, as a result, perhaps becoming confused, the secret is to list the numbers 1–4 (or as high as you need go) on a piece of paper with the corresponding coded letters beneath them. Thus the list would appear as:

    1 2 3 4 (5 6 7 8 9...)
    M A T E

However difficult the code might be, once you have done this the secrets of the code become much clearer.

    T E A M
    3 4 2 1

D is correct.

PRACTICE QUESTIONS

1 Which number comes next in the sequence?

2 5 8 11 **?**

A 12 **B** 14 **C** 13 **D** 15

2 Which number is missing in this sequence?

80 40 **?** 10 5

A 20 **B** 25 **C** 30 **D** 15

3 If the code for SEAT is X45Z, what is the code for TEA?

A Z4X **B** Z45

C X45 **D** Z54

4 In the following series of shapes, which would replace the question mark?

⇦ ↘ ⇧ ↗ ⇨ ↘ ⇩ **?**

A ⇩ **B** ↗ **C** ⇦ **D** ↗

5 Which shape would best fit into the gap in the following sequence?

⬠ **?** ◺ ◗

A ▭

B ◺

C ⬡

D ▭

6 In a sequence each number is 2 less than double the previous number. If the first number is 3, what is the fourth number?

A 6 **B** 8 **C** 10 **D** 16

7 If 6XH2 is DAUB and Z98V is GONE, what does 2H6ZV mean?

A BUDGE **B** BADGE

C BADGER **D** BOUND

8 In a code, each letter is represented by its number in the alphabet (so A = 1, B = 2, C = 3, and so on).

How would you write ZEBRA?

A 26.5.2.17.1 **B** 26.4.2.19.1

C 26.5.2.18.1 **D** 25.5.2.18.1

9 The numbers in the 'bricks' in this wall follow a certain pattern. Some numbers are missing.

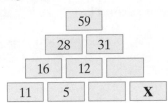

What number should be in the brick marked **X**?

A 12 **B** 16 **C** 19 **D** 21

☞ **Answers and explanations on pages 111–112**

Logical reasoning

ACTIVITY: This type of reasoning uses clear thinking and common sense. It might involve placing people or objects in order or determining which of a set of statements must be true or might not be true. It is very important to read the question carefully, more than once if necessary, to make sure you understand what is required. Don't rush: take time to think about what is needed and check the answer makes sense.

SAMPLE QUESTION 1

> Five cars—one black, one blue, one red, one silver and one white—are parked in a row. The first car is white. The red car is not last, nor is it next to the silver car. There is one car between the blue car and the red car.
>
>
> ?

Which car is **second last**?

A black   B blue   C red   D silver

STRATEGY

Read the question carefully and make sure you clearly understand what is needed. We are trying to find the car that is fourth in the line. In this type of question the answer is not immediately obvious. So work through the given information. In this way some options can be eliminated and the order gradually falls into place. Note that we haven't been asked to find the colour of all the cars but if we can do that quickly and easily it helps us to check we have the right answer.

To begin we are told the first car is white. This means the red car cannot be first and we are told it is not last. The red car must be one of the middle three cars. We are also told the red car is not next to the silver car or blue car. It can only be between the white and black cars. So the red car must be second and the black car must be third. The black car must be the one between the blue and red cars so the blue car must be fourth. The silver car will be last. The car that is second last is the blue car. **B is correct.**

white   red   black   blue   silver

SAMPLE QUESTION 2

> Luke, Jack and Dane are brothers. Jack is older than Luke and Dane is younger than Jack.

Which of these **must be true**?

A Luke is older than Dane.

B Jack is the oldest.

C Luke is the youngest.

D Dane is the youngest.

STRATEGY

Read the question carefully and take note of what is required. Here we are looking for the statement that **must** be true. This doesn't mean the other statements will necessarily be false. They might or might not be true. We need to consider each option and find the one that is definitely true. Perhaps a diagram might be helpful.

Here we are told Jack is older than Luke. We are also told Dane is younger than Jack. This means Jack is older than Dane. So Jack is older than both Luke and Dane and he must be the oldest.

There is no information about Dane's age compared to that of Luke. So Luke might be older than Dane but that is not a statement that **must** be true.

Either Luke or Dane must be the youngest. So one of the statements in options C and D will be true but we do not have enough information to say which one **must** be true.

The statement that **must** be true is 'Jack is the oldest'. **B is correct.**

PRACTICE QUESTIONS

1 Which answer is correct?

A All cats have 4 legs, some cats are black, therefore most cats are not black.

B All cats have 4 legs, some cats like cream, therefore most cats drink cream.

C All cats have 4 legs, most cats purr, therefore all cats have 4 legs and purr.

D All cats have 4 legs, most cats have tails, therefore most cats have 4 legs and a tail.

2 Sara is standing in a queue for the canteen with Tina, Karen, Chris and Gary. Gary is in front of her and Karen is behind her. Chris is ahead of Karen but behind Gary. Tina is ahead of Chris but behind Sara. What number is Sara in the queue?

A 1   B 4   C 3   D 2

3 This set of drawers holds T-shirts, underwear, socks and pyjamas.

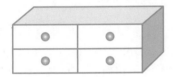

The underwear and pyjamas are diagonally opposite each other and the socks are at the top.

Which **must** be correct?

A The underwear is on top of the T-shirts.

B The pyjamas are on the bottom.

C The T-shirts are on the bottom.

D The underwear is beside the socks.

4 Two netball teams, the Ferns and the Roses, played three matches in a finals series to win a competition. The Roses won the first match, the Ferns won the last match and there were no ties or draws.

Which of these statements **must** be true?

A The Roses won the competition.

B The Ferns won a game immediately after the Roses won a game.

C The Ferns won the competition.

D The Roses won a game immediately after the Ferns won a game.

5 Five people—Emily, Freya, Harold, Patrick and Sarah—each have one of five adjoining rooms, numbered from 1 to 5, in a motel.

| 1 | 2 | 3 | 4 | 5 |

Sarah is in a higher-numbered room than Patrick and Emily is next to them both.

Freya is in a lower-numbered room than Harold but is not next to him.

Who is in room number 4?

A Sarah   B Harold

C Patrick   D Emily

☞ Answers and explanations on page 112

Solving problems

ACTIVITY: Some questions don't fall into particular categories and might be different to anything you have seen before so it is important to develop some skills for solving unfamiliar problems. The most important thing to do is to read the question carefully and take time to think. Don't rush. If unsure where to start, begin with working out what you know. Remember: With multiple-choice questions you can use the options to see which one works rather than work out the answer first.

SAMPLE QUESTION 1

> Every row, every column and both diagonals of this magic square add to the same amount. Some numbers are missing and have been replaced with P, Q, R, S and T.
>
> | 6 | P | Q |
> |---|---|---|
> | 1 | R | 9 |
> | 8 | S | T |

What number does P replace?

A 3 　　　 B 4 　　　 C 5 　　　 D 7

STRATEGY

Read the question carefully and understand what is required. The missing numbers need to be found. It isn't possible to find the answer immediately so first find what you can. Here every row, column and long diagonal adds to the same number. One column is complete so we can use that to find the amount that all rows and columns must add up to.

6 + 1 + 8 = 15 so the total of all rows, columns and long diagonals must be 15.

The second row has 1, R and 9. 1 + 9 = 10. The value of R must be 5 because 10 + 5 = 15.

Knowing the value of R we can now complete the diagonals. Finding the value of T will not easily help us find the required value of P. Finding the value of Q is the best option. 8 + 5 = 13. So Q must be 2 to add to 15.

From the top row 6 + P + 2 = 15. So P + 8 = 15, meaning P must be 7. **D is correct.**

The magic square can be filled in and we can check that all the rows, columns and diagonals add to 15.

6	7	2
1	5	9
8	3	4

SAMPLE QUESTION 2

> Rosie has some yellow, green and blue marbles. She has 8 of one colour, 7 of another and 5 of the third.

If Rosie has more yellow than green marbles and fewer green marbles than blue ones, which **must** be correct?

A　Rosie has 8 blue marbles.

B　Rosie has 8 yellow marbles.

C　Rosie has 5 green marbles.

D　Rosie has 7 blue marbles.

STRATEGY

When solving problems it is very important to read the question carefully to make sure you understand what is required. Here we need to sort through the given information and work out which one of the statements must be correct. Some of the other statements might be correct but we need the one that **must** be correct.

Rosie has 8 marbles of one colour, 7 of another and 5 of the third colour. She has more yellow than green marbles and fewer green marbles than blue ones so green is the colour of the least number of marbles. The statement that must be correct is that Rosie has 5 green marbles. Rosie has more yellow and more blue marbles than green marbles but there is no further information. So, Rosie might have 8 yellow marbles and she must have either 8 or 7 blue marbles, but we cannot say that any of the other options **must** be correct. **C is correct.**

PRACTICE QUESTIONS

1 Harvey bought 6 apples, each costing 70 cents. He also bought a watermelon. Harvey received $7.30 change from $20.00. How much was the watermelon?

A $7.50   B $7.80
C $8.20   D $8.50

2 Cora used some of the coins she had in her money box to pay to go to the movies. She had the following coins:

$2 $2 50c 50c 50c 20c 10c 5c 5c

How many coins would she need to pay the exact price of $3.65?

A 4   B 5   C 6   D 7

3 Two numbers added together equal 20. When one is subtracted from the other, the answer is 4.

What are the two numbers?

A 15 and 5   B 11 and 7
C 16 and 4   D 12 and 8

4 Farid's mother and father went on a sea cruise. They saved $2500 for the whole trip, of which the voyage cost $1900, the entertainments cost $150, the tours of ports they visited cost $240 and the games they played cost $155. There was some of their $2500 left over. How much?

A $145   B $255
C $55   D $65

5 Last week, out of his pocket money, Shane spent $3.50 on travel, $12.30 on food and $8.50 on a haircut. A friend also paid him back the $1.75 he owed him. He ended the week with $2.45.

How much pocket money did he get?

A $25.00   B $28.50
C $30.00   D $20.00

6 A window cleaner stands on the middle rung of a ladder washing windows. He climbs up 3 rungs to the next set of windows, then he sees a window he has missed and goes back down 5 rungs.

Following that he climbs up 7 rungs to wash the rest, then climbs 6 more rungs to the top of the ladder.

How many rungs did the ladder have?

A 23   B 25   C 21   D 24

7 In this magic square the numbers in every row, every column and both diagonals add up to 24 but some of the numbers are missing.

What number will go in the space marked with an X?

5		
	8	X
	4	

A 6   B 7   C 9   D 10

8 Mabel wants to buy a set of mugs. There are 12 different mugs in the set and she wants to buy them all. Mabel knows that four different local shops are selling the mugs but all have different prices and three have special offers.

Shop owner	Normal price per mug	Special offer
Alice	$7	
Max	$10	Buy 2 get 1 free
Penny	$9	Buy 3 get 1 free
Thomas	$8	Buy 2 get 1 more for half price

From which shop owner(s) would Mabel buy 12 mugs for the least amount?

A Alice only   B Penny only

C Thomas only   D Either Thomas or Max

☞ Answers and explanations on pages 112–113

Working with shapes

ACTIVITY: Spatial reasoning means the ability to visualise and understand both two-dimensional and three-dimensional shapes and objects. This might mean identifying basic shapes and objects, recognising their properties, and manipulating shapes and objects in different orientations or forms.

SAMPLE QUESTION 1

Vera has a regular hexagon. She draws one straight line across the hexagon and divides it into a pentagon and another shape.

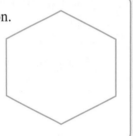

Which of these could be the other shape?

    X   a triangle

    Y   a quadrilateral

    Z   another pentagon

A   X only   B   Y only

C   X and Y only   D   Y and Z only

E   X, Y and Z

STRATEGY

This question tests the student's understanding of the names of different shapes as well as the ability to visualise and manipulate them.

Here we begin with a hexagon, a six-sided shape. It is to be divided into two parts, one part being a pentagon (a five-sided shape). There are different possible outcomes and all need to be considered.

The easiest method is to imagine a line drawn across the hexagon in different places. Note: The hexagon does not have to be divided in half.

Among others, the hexagon can be divided into a pentagon and a triangle, a pentagon and a quadrilateral (four-sided shape) or two pentagons. **E is correct.**

SAMPLE QUESTION 2

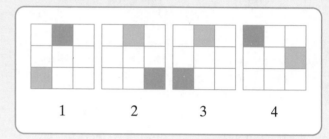

    1   2   3   4

Two of the above four shapes are the same except that one of the two has been rotated through a quarter of a turn (90°). Which two?

A   1 and 2   B   2 and 3

C   3 and 4   D   2 and 4

E   1 and 4

STRATEGY

The key parts of the pattern are the two shaded (dark blue and blue) squares within the large squares. They must stay in the same position in relation to each other when the large square is turned around (rotated). For a start, 1 can be ruled out since it is the only one with the dark blue square not in a corner.

Now, imagine turning each of the other squares. If 2 moves, the dark blue square will match the dark blue square in 3 but the blue squares will not match. If 3 moves, both the dark blue square and the blue square will match 4.

C is correct.

PRACTICE QUESTIONS

1 Which figure below shows the result when this shape is reflected in a vertical mirror?

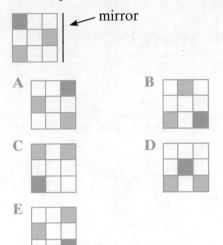

2 Katrina looks at a sign on a waiting room wall and sees: EXIT ➡

Then she sees the sign in the mirror on the opposite wall. How does the sign **look**?

3 Here is a figure:

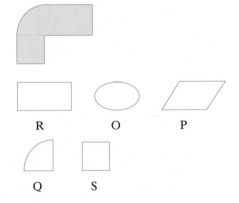

■ Which of these shapes have been joined to make the shaded figure?

A R + S + P   B S + O + R
C S + P + Q   D S + R + Q
E Q + R + P

4 How many squares are there in the figure?

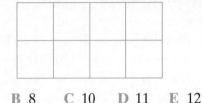

A 6   B 8   C 10   D 11   E 12

5 How many of the small shape will fit into the large one?

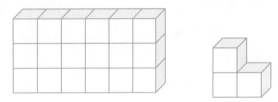

A 4   B 5   C 6   D 7   E 8

6 On a normal dice the numbers on the opposite faces add to 7. This is not a normal dice.

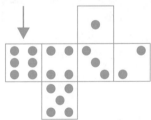

What will the numbers on the face pointed to by the arrow and its opposite face add up to?

A 7   B 8   C 9   D 10   E 11

☞ **Answers and explanations on pages 113–114**

Working with numbers

ACTIVITY: Numbers are such an important part of our world and we all need to have a basic understanding of our number system. We also need to understand basic arithmetical processes and be confident working with numbers. Reasoning questions might require a little more thought.

SAMPLE QUESTION 1

> Ben and Tom both choose cards from a pack that has all the whole numbers less than 10. Ben's cards show 8, 3 and 5. Tom's cards are 4, 7 and 1. Using each card once, Ben makes the largest three-digit number that he can with his cards and Tom makes the smallest three-digit number that he can with his.

What is the difference between those two three-digit numbers?

A 714   **B** 706   **C** 688   **D** 356   **E** 483

STRATEGY

Read the question carefully and make sure you understand what is required. Three-digit numbers will be formed by the numbers on the cards. Remember: To find the difference between two numbers we subtract the smaller from the larger.

Here Ben has the numbers 8, 3 and 5 on his cards. The largest three-digit number he can form must begin with the largest of those cards, 8. The second digit in Ben's number must be the next largest card, 5. So Ben's number must be 853.

Tom has the numbers 4, 7 and 1 on his cards. The smallest three-digit number he can make will begin with the smallest card, 1. The second digit will be the next smallest card, 4. So Tom's number will be 147.

To find the difference: 853 – 147 = 706.
B is correct.

SAMPLE QUESTION 2

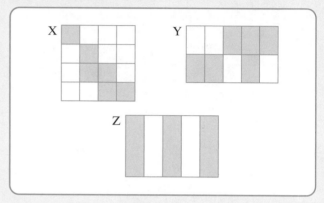

Which of these rectangles has/have $\frac{6}{10}$ shaded?

A X only   **B** Y only

C Z only   **D** Y and Z only

E X, Y and Z

STRATEGY

In this question we need to consider all three rectangles because the answer could be any combination of X, Y and Z. We are looking for rectangles where 6 out of every 10 spaces will be shaded.

Here X is a square (and also a rectangle) divided into 16 equal-sized squares. 6 squares are shaded and 10 are not. The fraction of shaded squares is 6 out of 16 not 6 out of 10. So X is not an answer.

Rectangle Y is divided into 10 equal parts. 6 of those parts are shaded. So Y is an answer. Note: It is important that the parts are equal size.

Rectangle Z is divided into 5 equal parts. Three of those parts are shaded. $\frac{3}{5} = \frac{6}{10}$. An easy way to see this is to imagine a horizontal line drawn across the middle of the rectangle so that there would then be 6 out of 10 parts shaded. So Z is an answer. **D is correct.**

PRACTICE QUESTIONS

1 If I visit the greengrocer and buy 2 kg of potatoes which are $2.50 a kg, 2 kg of carrots at $1.50 a kilogram and 2 rockmelons at $1.50 each, how much change will I get from $15?

A $4.00   B $4.50
C $5.00   D $5.50
E $6.00

2 Mary took her three brothers to a concert. The cost to go in is $5.00 per person but, because they were under age, her brothers could go in for half-price. How would you calculate how much Mary had to pay altogether?

A $4 \times \frac{1}{2} \times \$5.00$

B $\$5.00 + 3 \times \frac{1}{2} \times \$5.00$

C $\$5.00 + 4 \times \frac{1}{2} \times \$5.00$

D $4 \times \$5.00 - \frac{1}{2} \times \$5.00$

E $4 \times \$5.00 - 3 \times \frac{1}{2}$

3 What number is seven hundreds more than 82 569?

A 82 769   B 83 169
C 83 269   D 83 369
E 89 569

4 Peter is twice as old as Marco. Ken is 9 and is one year older than Peter. How old is Marco?

A 5   B 3   C 8   D 6   E 4

5 Which process do I use to find the number of hundreds in 4000?

A $4000 \times 100 = \square$

B $4000 \div 100 = \square$

C $400 \div 100 = \square$

D $100 \div 4000 = \square$

E $4000 \div 400 = \square$

☞ Answers and explanations on page 114

6 Imogen and Vincent are playing a game with marbles. Altogether there are 24 marbles and Imogen has twice as many as Vincent. How many marbles does Imogen have?

A 6   B 8   C 12   D 16   E 18

7 Which of these rectangles has/have $\frac{3}{5}$ shaded?

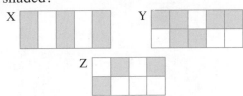

A X only   B Z only
C X and Y only   D X and Z only
E X, Y and Z

8 Morgan is making a pattern with black and white tiles. Each row of the pattern uses 3 white and 4 black tiles. The finished pattern uses 28 black tiles. How many white tiles were used?

A 12   B 16   C 20   D 21   E 24

Working with measurements

ACTIVITY: Being able to measure the size of things is very important and we must also have a basic understanding of the units we use to measure. Kilometres (km), metres (m), centimetres (cm) and millimetres (mm) are the most common units used for measuring length. Kilograms (kg), grams (g) and milligrams (mg) are used for measuring mass (weight). Litres (L) and millilitres (mL) are used for measuring capacity. We also use square units to measure area, most commonly square centimetres (cm^2) and square metres (m^2).

SAMPLE QUESTION 1

Two jugs both have water in them as shown.

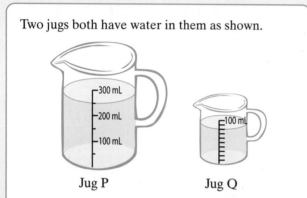

Jug P   Jug Q

Jug P holds 300 mL when full. Some of the water in jug Q is used to fill jug P.

How much water will be left in jug Q?

A 30 mL   B 40 mL

C 50 mL   D 60 mL

E 70 mL

STRATEGY

This question tests the ability to read and understand the scale on the jugs. The amount of water in each jug needs to be found and then the question itself can be considered.

On jug P the scale is marked in 50-mL increments, with each 100 mL given. So the jug originally has 250 mL. As it holds 300 mL when full, another 50 mL will be needed to fill it.

Jug Q has a scale that goes to 100 mL. There are 10 marks on the scale so each mark is $100 \div 10$ or 10 mL. So jug Q originally holds 80 mL. If 50 mL is taken out, 30 mL will remain. **A is correct.**

SAMPLE QUESTION 2

A rectangle with width 3 cm has a perimeter with the same length as that of this triangle.

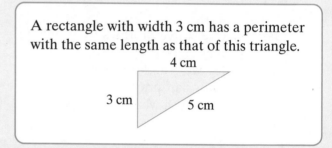

What would be the length of the rectangle?

A 3 cm   B 4 cm   C 5 cm   D 6 cm   E 7 cm

STRATEGY

Perimeter is the distance around the outside of an object. The perimeter of the triangle can easily be found by adding the lengths of the sides. A rectangle has two pairs of equal sides so its perimeter is equal to twice the length plus twice the width.

Here the perimeter of the triangle is $(3 + 4 + 5)$ cm or 12 cm. The question therefore means find the length of a rectangle with perimeter 12 cm if the width is 3 cm. Twice the width is 2×3 cm or 6 cm. As $12 - 6 = 6$, twice the length must also be 6 cm. This means the length must also be 3 cm. **A is correct.**

Note: A square is a rectangle. It is a special rectangle with all of its sides equal but it is still a rectangle.

PRACTICE QUESTIONS

1 Rachel has a piece of centimetre-squared paper. She shades a pattern on the paper.

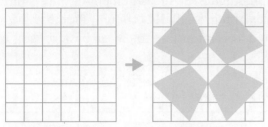

What is the area of the paper that is shaded?

A 16 cm²   B 18 cm²

C 20 cm²   D 24 cm²

E 32 cm²

2 A grid is marked out on a field as shown. Each square on the grid has a side length of 10 m. Rachel is at the centre of the grid marked R and moves according to the instructions below.

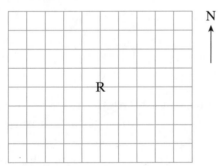

Move 30 m south then 30 m east. Next move 20 m north, then 40 m west and finally 10 m north.

How far is Rachel from the point R where she started?

A 10 m B 20 m C 30 m D 40 m E 130 m

3 Sophie needs 350 mL of milk in a recipe. She has the amount in this jug.

After using the milk in her recipe, how many millilitres will Sophie have left in the jug?

A 200   B 250   C 300   D 350   E 650

4 What is the perimeter (the distance all the way around the outside) of this shape?

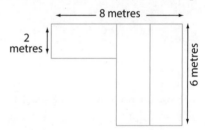

A 28 metres   B 24 metres

C 20 metres   D 26 metres

E 32 metres

5 At her school athletics carnival, Sharma enters in the 75 m, the 200 m, the 400 m and the 800 m races, as well as the three-legged race. If she ran $1\frac{1}{2}$ km altogether, how far did she run in the three-legged race?

A 75 m   B 35 m

C 55 m   D 25 m

E 45 m

☞ **Answers and explanations on pages 114–115**

Working with time and dates

ACTIVITY: Working with time can be very confusing because there are so many different variables. There are different forms in which time can be expressed, such as half past ten or 10:30. There is the need to use terms such as am or pm as well as noon, midday and midnight. The measurement of time is different to other measurements because the units are not multiples of ten. Similarly, different months have different numbers of days so dates can also be complicated. It is important to have a basic idea of how to approach questions.

SAMPLE QUESTION 1

> On Saturday Quan was allowed to go riding on his bike with friends from 10:30 am till 2:00 pm.

How long was this?

A $1\frac{1}{2}$ hours   **B** 2 hours

C $2\frac{1}{2}$ hours   **D** 3 hours

E $3\frac{1}{2}$ hours

STRATEGY

Time can sometimes be a tricky concept, especially as so many people have digital watches or smartphones, making it a little more difficult to 'picture' the time passing.

The easiest way to find lengths of time is to count in stages. Here the question is simply asking how long it is from 10:30 in the morning until 2:00 in the afternoon.

From 10:30 until 11:00 is half an hour, then from 11 to 12, 12 to 1 and 1 to 2 is another three hours. So Quan was allowed to ride his bike for $3\frac{1}{2}$ hours. **E is correct.**

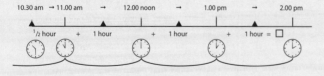

SAMPLE QUESTION 2

> A circus is going to appear in town. The first show will be on Friday 3 May and the last one will be on 19 May. There will be shows every night of the week, except for Mondays.

How many shows will there be?

A 13   **B** 14   **C** 15   **D** 16   **E** 17

STRATEGY

This question is not quite straightforward because it involves a few different parts. It is asking how many times the circus will perform. Before this can be answered we need to find the length of time between the two dates and determine the days of the week. Counting forwards by 7s is the best way to begin.

First if 3 May is a Friday, then so is 10 May and 17 May. This means 19 May will be a Sunday. So the circus will be in town for 2 full weeks from Friday 3 May until Thursday 16 May, followed by 3 more days. Each week there are shows every night except for Mondays. So there are 6 shows each week. In 2 weeks there will be 2 × 6 or 12 shows. There will also be shows on Friday 17 May, Saturday 18 May and Sunday 19 May. So that is another 3 shows. As 12 + 3 = 15, there will be 15 shows altogether. **C is correct.**

PRACTICE QUESTIONS

1 Sally goes to visit her friend, Victoria, and her mother tells her to be home in $3\frac{3}{4}$ hours to tidy her room. If she leaves home 15 minutes before 12 noon, what time does she have to be home by?

A 3:30 pm B 3:15 pm
C 4 pm D 2:45 pm
E 3:45 pm

2 Perth is 2 hours behind Sydney and New Zealand is 2 hours ahead of Sydney. What time will it be in Perth when it is 10 am in New Zealand?

A 2:00 pm B 12:00 noon
C 6:00 am D 8:00 am
E 10 am

3 The time in London is 10 hours behind the time in Sydney. What time will it be in London when it is 7:00 am on Wednesday in Sydney?

A 7:00 pm on Wednesday
B 9:00 pm on Wednesday
C 9:00 pm on Tuesday
D 9:00 am on Tuesday
E 5:00 pm on Thursday

4 If 7 March is a Tuesday, what day of the week will 4 April be?

A Monday B Tuesday
C Wednesday D Thursday
E Friday

5 Siva's parents leave for a weekend in Melbourne at 6:30 pm on Friday and arrive home on Monday at 7:30 am. How many hours have they been gone for?

A 49 hours B 53 hours
C 73 hours D 63 hours
E 61 hours

6 A one-day cricket international lasts for seven and a half hours. If it starts at 10:30 am, at what time will it finish?

A 5:00 pm B 8:00 pm
C 4:00 am D 7:00 pm
E 6:00 pm

7 Throughout June an opera will be performed on Friday, Saturday and Sunday nights and on Wednesday afternoons. If 1 June is a Friday, how many times will the opera be performed in June?

A 17 B 18 C 19 D 20 E 21

8 During the week, Keith spends 1 hour travelling to and from school. On Wednesday he goes to football and this adds on an extra 30 minutes. How much time does Keith spend travelling each week?

A 6 hours

B $5\frac{1}{4}$ hours

C $7\frac{1}{2}$ hours

D $5\frac{1}{2}$ hours

E $10\frac{1}{2}$ hours

☞ Answers and explanations on page 115

Working with graphs

ACTIVITY: Often information is shown in a graph. It is important to be able to read and interpret the information given. There are many different types of graphs, the most common for this age group being the column graph. All graphs should clearly show what is being presented without the need for lots of accompanying explanations. A graph gives a quick visual picture of the data.

SAMPLE QUESTION 1

This graph shows the total number of cars of different colours sold by a company during one month.

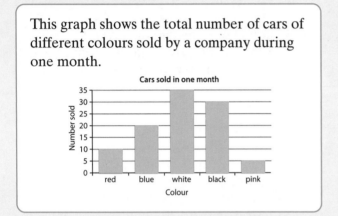

How many **more** black cars were sold than blue and pink combined?

A 5   B 10   C 15   D 20   E 25

STRATEGY

The important part of working with graphs is to be able to read and interpret the information that is given in graphical form.

Here there is a different column for each of five different colours, as shown on the horizontal axis. The height of the columns give the number of cars of that colour that have been sold in the month. The vertical axis shows that each line is 5 cars.

So reading the graph we can see that the column labelled black has a height of 30, meaning there were 30 black cars sold. The number of blue cars sold is 20 and the number of pink cars sold is 5. Now, 20 + 5 = 25 so the total of blue and pink combined is 25. 30 – 25 = 5 so there were 5 more black cars sold than blue and pink combined. **A is correct.**

SAMPLE QUESTION 2

A group of children were asked how many siblings (brothers and sisters) they each had. The graph shows the results.

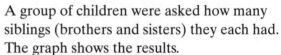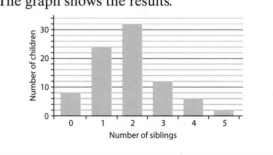

How many of the children had **more than 2** siblings?

A 3   B 10   C 12   D 20   E 32

STRATEGY

It is important to understand what the graph is about and what the question requires. Here both the axes involve numbers so care is needed to avoid confusion. The horizontal axis gives the possible numbers of siblings (brothers and sisters). They range between none and five. The vertical axis gives the number of children from the group who had that many siblings. The numbers on the vertical axis go up by tens. There are five marks between those tens so each line means another two. We count by 2s to find the numbers. So, for example, 24 children have one brother or sister.

The question asks how many children have more than 2 siblings. 32 children have 2 siblings but we want to know how many have more than 2. 12 children have 3 siblings, 6 children have 4 siblings and 2 children have 5 siblings. 12 + 6 + 2 = 20. So 20 children have more than 2 siblings. **D is correct.**

PRACTICE QUESTIONS

1 The column graph below tells us the different times of day that a group of 100 workers leave for work each morning.

How many of the workers leave for work before 7 am?

A 25   B 10   C 45   D 35   E 20

2 This graph shows the numbers of items sold at the canteen on Wednesday.

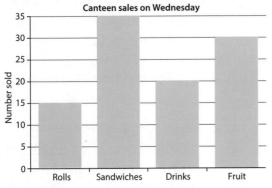

The canteen sold twice as many of one item as of one other item on Wednesday. Which were the two items?

A drinks and rolls

B fruit and drinks

C sandwiches and drinks

D fruit and rolls

E rolls and sandwiches

3 In Ticktack Primary School Mrs Nath, the sport teacher, counted the number of children playing different sports and came up with the following figures:

cricket	swimming	athletics	softball	tennis	gymnastics
40	60	30	50	20	40

Mr Jensen, the other sport teacher, preferred to give this information to the principal in the form of a graph. His graph is shown below.

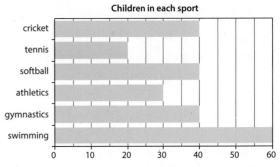

However, he got the number for one of the sports wrong. Which sport was that?

A cricket

B gymnastics

C softball

D athletics

E tennis

☞ Answers and explanations on page 115

SAMPLE TEST

Read the text below then answer the questions.

The Wild Swans

Far away in the land to which the swallows fly when it is winter, dwelt a king who had eleven sons, and one daughter, named Eliza. The eleven brothers were princes, and each went to school with a star on his breast, and a sword by his side. They wrote with diamond pencils on gold slates, and learnt their lessons so quickly and read so easily that every one might know they were princes. Their sister Eliza sat on a little stool of plate-glass, and had a book full of pictures, which had cost as much as half a kingdom. Oh, these children were indeed happy, but it was not to remain so always. Their father, who was king of the country, married a very wicked queen, who did not love the poor children at all. They knew this from the very first day after the wedding. In the palace there were great festivities, and the children played at receiving company; but instead of having, as usual, all the cakes and apples that were left, she gave them some sand in a tea-cup, and told them to pretend it was cake. The week after, she sent little Eliza into the country to a peasant and his wife, and then she told the king so many untrue things about the young princes, that he gave himself no more trouble respecting them.

'Go out into the world and get your own living,' said the queen. 'Fly like great birds, who have no voice.' But she could not make them ugly as she wished, for they were turned into eleven beautiful wild swans. Then, with a strange cry, they flew through the windows of the palace, over the park, to the forest beyond. It was early morning when they passed the peasant's cottage, where their sister Eliza lay asleep in her room. They hovered over the roof, twisted their long necks and flapped their wings, but no one heard them or saw them, so they were at last obliged to fly away, high up in the clouds; and over the wide world they flew till they came to a thick, dark wood, which stretched far away to the seashore.

[…]

At fifteen Eliza returned home, but when the queen saw how beautiful she was, she became full of spite and hatred towards her. Willingly would she have turned her into a swan, like her brothers, but she did not dare to do so yet, because the king wished to see his daughter. Early one morning the queen went into the bath-room; it was built of marble, and had soft cushions, trimmed with the most beautiful tapestry. She took three toads with her, and kissed them, and said to one, 'When Eliza comes to the bath, seat yourself upon her head, that she may become as stupid as you are.' Then she said to another, 'Place yourself on her forehead, that she may become as ugly as you are, and that her father may not know her.' 'Rest on her heart,' she whispered to the third, 'then she will have evil inclinations, and suffer in consequence.' So she put the toads into the clear water, and they turned green immediately. She next called Eliza, and helped her to undress and get into the bath. As Eliza dipped her head under the water, one of the toads sat on her hair, a second on her forehead, and a third on her breast, but she did not seem to notice them, and when she rose out of the water, there were three red poppies floating upon it. Had not the creatures been venomous or been kissed by the witch, they would have been changed into red roses. At all events they became flowers, because they had rested on Eliza's head, and on her heart. She was too good and too innocent for witchcraft to have any power over her. When the wicked queen saw this, she rubbed

SAMPLE TEST

her face with walnut-juice; then she tangled her beautiful hair and smeared it with disgusting ointment, till it was quite impossible to recognize the beautiful Eliza.

When her father saw her, he was much shocked, and declared she was not his daughter. No one but the watch-dog and the swallows knew her; and they were only poor animals, and could say nothing. Then poor Eliza wept, and thought of her eleven brothers, who were all away. Sorrowfully, she stole away from the palace, and walked, the whole day, over fields and moors, till she came to the great forest.

From 'The Wild Swans' by Hans Christian Andersen

For questions **1–5**, choose the option (**A**, **B**, **C** or **D**) which you think best answers the question.

1 What is the most likely reason the queen agreed to marry the king?

A She loved him dearly.

B She wanted to be a stepmother.

C He was enormously rich.

D He had a good reputation.

2 Why does the king stop caring about his sons?

A He believed the queen's lies about them.

B He'd seen them fly away.

C He was jealous of how clever they were.

D He had always preferred Eliza.

3 The swans hovered above the peasant's cottage because they

A hoped to find rest there.

B wanted to be in touch with Eliza.

C had a message for the peasant and his wife.

D hoped to find food for their journey.

4 Which of the features of this text is least typical of a fairytale?

A the wicked stepmother

B a great forest

C obedient children who are treated badly

D animals that turn into flowers

5 You predict the queen will be punished because

A she is not very clever.

B she doesn't have a fairy godmother.

C good always overcomes evil in fairytales.

D Eliza will want her revenge.

☞ **Answers and explanations on pages 116–118**

SAMPLE TEST

Read the poem below by Maura Pierlot then answer the questions.

Today

Hey Mum, I asked,
can I play in the park?
Tomorrow is better,
she said. It's too dark.

But I'd rather play now.
Please let me, okay?
Tomorrow, I told her,
is too far away.

Today won't be with us
for long, Mum did muse.
Tomorrow, today
will be yesterday's news.

Mum, that makes sense
because just yesterday,
today was tomorrow.
So now can I play?

© Maura Pierlot; reproduced with permission

For questions **6–9**, choose the option (**A**, **B**, **C** or **D**) which you think best answers the question.

6 Which two stanzas deal only with the daughter's words and thoughts?

   A one and two
   B two and three
   C three and four
   D two and four

7 The daughter tries to persuade her mother to do what she wants by being

   A reasonable.
   B rude.
   C unpleasant.
   D polite.

8 Why does Mum begin to change her mind?

   A Her daughter nagged her.
   B She didn't like to refuse.
   C She thinks about the nature of time.
   D She is afraid of her daughter's anger.

9 Does the poem suggest the daughter has won the argument?

   A Yes, it seems her mother will probably allow her to play.
   B No, her mother remains unconvinced.
   C Yes, she has definitely persuaded her Mum to let her play.
   D No, her mother is unlikely to change her mind.

☞ **Answers and explanations on pages 116–118**

SAMPLE TEST

Read the text below then answer the questions.

Choose from the sentences (**A–D**) the one which fits each gap (**10–14**). There is one extra sentence which you do not need to use.

The Loch Ness Monster

A strange aquatic creature carved in a stone outcrop by the Picts, early inhabitants of Scotland, is thought to be an early 'picture' of Nessie, the Loch Ness Monster. There was also a written account of a sighting of the Monster on the shores of the Loch in a biography of St Columba, an Irish missionary, written about 1500 years ago by his successor. **10** _____ He ordered the Monster, in God's name, to return immediately to the Loch—an order we are told it obeyed!

Since that time, every now and then, someone claims to glimpse the Monster as it rises from the murky waters of the lake. **11** _____ Soon after this, there was another reported sighting. As a result, London newspapers sent reporters to stake out the scene. *The Daily Mail* even hired a big-game hunter and sent him to Loch Ness to capture the beast. **12** _____ Casts of the footprints were sent back to London and it was found, alas, that they were part of a hoax. The footprints were those of a stuffed hippopotamus's foot planted in the soil to make it seem as if a Monster had walked there.

This didn't end speculation that the Monster existed. **13** _____ Perhaps an aquatic plesiosaur or even an archeocyte, a primitive whale with a serpentine neck? Others argue there is no way a dinosaur could have survived because the lake was frozen over during the ice ages. They suggest people are tricked into believing they see a Monster when what they see is a disturbance in the water caused by cold river water flowing into the warmer Loch.

Scientists have attempted to settle the question by using sonar equipment to search the deep. **14** _____ However, they admit they have found moving underwater objects they can't yet explain. Intriguing!

A   On May 2, 1933, for example, the *Inverness Courier* quoted that a local couple said they had seen 'an enormous animal rolling and plunging' on its surface.

B   A photo taken in 1934 led some people to think that Nessie must be a lone survivor of a dinosaur family.

C   He found footprints of the animal, which led to a frenzy of excitement.

D   So far they have failed to find the Monster.

E   The biography included mention of St Columba coming across a large beast who was attacking a man there.

F   It is usually described as a creature that raises its head and parts of its enormous body above the lake's surface.

☞ **Answers and explanations on pages 116–118**

SAMPLE TEST

Read the four texts below on the theme of spiders.

For questions **15–20**, choose the option (**A**, **B**, **C** or **D**) which you think best answers the question.

Which text ...

15 is about a spider with a name that reflects the shape of its web? _____

16 suggests pride comes before a fall? _____

17 refers to a unique way of travelling long distances? _____

18 mentions a particular legend? _____

19 gives the most general information about spiders? _____

20 refers to a gender difference in a particular type of spider? _____

TEXT A

The spider woman, Arachne, wove the most beautiful tapestries. They were admired by everyone. 'My tapestries are the best in the world. I need no help from the Goddess Athena,' she boasted. 'Do you think you are better than Athena?' asked an old woman in rags who was among the crowd. 'Certainly,' replied Arachne. 'Then let us have a contest,' said the old woman. Her rags fell away and Athena was revealed. 'I told you I was better,' Arachne said proudly as their tapestries were compared. 'You may be better but you are without respect. You need to be taught a lesson,' the Goddess replied. Arachne felt herself shrinking slowly. Her hands disappeared. They were replaced with eight long, hairy fingers. That night Arachne made a beautiful shining web. When her father noticed the web, he called his servant to get rid of it. What a harsh lesson for Arachne!

TEXT B

Spiders have lived on earth for millions of years. They are the largest order of the Arachnida, an order that also includes dust mites, ticks and scorpions. The word 'arachnid' comes from the Greek word for 'spider'. Spiders have eight jointed legs but, unlike insects, they don't have wings or antennae. They have two body parts: a combined head and thorax, and an abdomen. Their fangs are used to inject venom and their spinnerets used to exude silk.

Spiders are carnivorous and eat insects, other spiders and even small animals such as lizards. They can't chew so they suck in their prey after spitting enzymes outside their body to break them down.

They live all over the world except for the polar regions. Some young spiders move about by a process called ballooning. They put out their silk threads which are then caught by the wind. They can be carried nearby or over long distances across land and sea.

☞ **Answers and explanations on pages 116–118**

SAMPLE TEST

TEXT C

Daddy long legs is the common name for the Pholcidae family of the Arachnida. They earned their name because of their extremely long, very thin legs in relation to their very small bodies. They are able to shed a leg automatically if that leg is under attack. If this happens, and it is quite common, they have to learn a whole new way of walking.

Daddy long legs like dark, moist places and usually choose to live inside buildings. They can be very at home in the corner of a ceiling or perhaps under a table or in the corner of your shower.

Some people believe that if you kill a daddy long legs (by mistake, of course, as they won't hurt you) it will rain the next day. There is also an old legend that if you see a daddy long legs in the evening, good luck and happiness are sure to follow.

TEXT D

There are about 40 different species of funnel-web spider. They like to build funnel-shaped webs that they use as burrows. They add silk trip lines to their burrows to protect themselves from intruders. Their webs are usually located in moist, damp places, often under logs or rocks, or hidden in bushland or gardens.

Funnel-web spiders tend to be of medium size with the males being more lightly built than the females. Some species have highly toxic venom and there have been human deaths recorded from the bites of the male. They hunt mainly at night either by wandering about or by sitting just inside the entrance of the web and then pouncing on prey that walks across its silk lines. If they fall into swimming pools they can stay alive for hours.

An antivenom is available to treat human victims of their bites. Immediate first aid is also recommended, such as putting pressure on an affected limb and binding it tightly from the bitten area to above the bite.

SAMPLE TEST

1 Katrina looks at a sign on a waiting room wall and sees: `TOILETS ▶`

Then she sees the sign in the mirror on the opposite wall. How does the sign look?

A `◀ TOILETS` B `▶ TOILETS`
C `◀ STELIOT` D `◀ ƧTƎ⅃IOT`

2 A donkey is smaller than a horse but has longer ears and a shorter mane. A donkey's tail is more like a cow's tail than a horse's tail. A mule is a cross between a horse and a donkey. Mules are taller than donkeys with smaller ears and tails like horses. A mule is born to a male donkey and a female horse. Mules themselves cannot breed.

Owen: 'That animal suckling its baby can't be a horse because it's got a short mane, a tail like a cow and big ears. It might be a donkey.'

Amar: 'That donkey is suckling its baby. The baby must be a mule.'

If the information in the box is true, whose reasoning is correct?

A Owen only

B Amar only

C Both Owen and Amar

D Neither Owen nor Amar

3 Four boys took part in a spelling competition. They were each asked to spell 30 words. For the first test the boys did not know what the words might be but for the second test the boys were given a few minutes to study the words before the test. All the boys did better on the second test than the first.

Name	First test	Second test
Abraham	21	26
James	23	27
Paul	17	23
Thomas	18	25

Who improved their score the most?

A Abraham   B James

C Paul   D Thomas

4 Mallory is an experienced juggler. She says it usually takes a month for beginner jugglers to master the three-ball cascade, which is the basic juggling trick of keeping three balls in the air.

If Mallory is correct, which one of the following statements is true?

A Everyone who practises juggling for a month will master the three-ball cascade.

B No-one who practises juggling for less than a month will master the three-ball cascade.

C Some of the people who practise juggling for less than a month will master the three-ball cascade.

D Only the learners who've had less than a month of practice will manage to master the three-ball cascade.

☞ **Answers and explanations on pages 118–120**

SAMPLE TEST

5 Dominoes from a set have been used to create this square, with one domino missing. No number is repeated in any row, column or diagonal. Each domino is only used once in the square, although not all dominoes in the set are used. Which of these could be the missing domino?

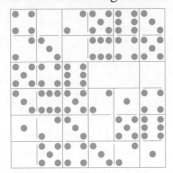

A   B

C   D

6 Which two squares have the same five shapes? (They might be turned over or around.)

  1   2   3   4

A 1 and 3   B 1 and 4
C 2 and 3   D 3 and 4

7 Karim wants to be a professional drummer. Drummers need excellent coordination because they use all four limbs at the same time. It usually takes years of study and practice to become a professional drummer but I think Karim will succeed faster than most because he is very determined.

Which one of these statements, if true, weakens the above argument?

A Drumming takes a great deal of physical effort.

B Karim's neighbours don't like him to make a lot of noise.

C Drumming is good exercise and helps to relieve stress.

D Karim has poor coordination.

8 **Leon**: 'Twenty-two residents at Grandad's aged-care home own electric wheelchairs. Twenty-two electric wheelchairs are parked in the parking area this afternoon so no-one who owns a wheelchair has gone out this afternoon.'

Which one of the following sentences shows the mistake Leon has made?

A If you own an electric wheelchair, you can take it out when you leave the home.

B Some of the people who own electric wheelchairs like to go for trips around the local community.

C If you own an electric wheelchair, you are required to park it in the parking area.

D Just because you own an electric wheelchair does not mean you always take it when you leave the home.

☞ **Answers and explanations on pages 118–120**

SAMPLE TEST

9 The circus will be performing on Thursday, Friday and Saturday nights each week beginning on Thursday 6 January and finishing on 28 January. There will also be Sunday afternoon performances on 16 and 23 January.

How many performances will there be altogether?

A 11 **B** 12 **C** 13 **D** 14

10 Lily's class was told to vote for the poem they would recite at the school assembly. Their choices were 'Triantiwontigongolope', 'Jim who was eaten by a lion' or The owl and the pussycat'. Each child was allowed two votes. They could not vote for the same poem twice. The vote would only be approved if one poem came out a clear winner with every child voting for it. If this didn't happen, the teacher would choose the poem. Every poem got at least one vote.

Knowing one of the following would allow us to know the result of the vote. Which one is it?

A Everyone voted for either 'The owl and the pussycat' or 'Triantiwontigongolope', or both.

B 'Jim who was eaten by a lion' was the most popular vote

C No-one voted for both 'Jim who was eaten by a lion' and 'Triantiwontigongolope'.

D Only two people voted for 'Triantiwontigongolope'.

11 This is the net of a cube.

When the net is folded, what will be on the face opposite the face with the star?

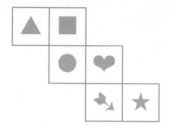

A triangle **B** square
C circle **D** heart

12 Alice, Erica, Hannah, Ilona, Maisie and Nadine are sitting at a round table. Alice is directly opposite Ilona. Nadine is next to Hannah.

Which must be true?

A Erica is next to Alice.

B Maisie is next to Erica.

C Ilona is next to Hannah.

D Nadine is next to Maisie.

☞ **Answers and explanations on pages 118–120**

SAMPLE TEST

13 A scientist said: 'The fossil remains of a Stegouros elengassen dinosaur, discovered in Chile in South America, tell us that this dinosaur had a tail shaped like a club. It's likely it swung its tail from side to side to ward off predators. It would have been fierce in battle.'

Which one of these statements, if true, best supports the scientist's claim?

A Its tail had sharp blades embedded along the sides.

B Its mouth was shaped like a beak so it was a plant eater.

C Its back had a bony, lumpy, bumpy coat of armour.

D It was a fairly small dinosaur.

14

Jaala has a dog called Yoda. Whenever she feeds Yoda pumpkin, he gets diarrhoea. Whenever he gets diarrhoea, Mum says he's not allowed in the car. Whenever he's not allowed in the car, he digs holes in the lawn.

Dean: 'I know Yoda dug holes in the lawn yesterday. He must have had diarrhoea'.

Braiden: 'If Yoda gets diarrhoea tomorrow, he won't be allowed in the car to go on our picnic.'

If the information in the box is true, whose reasoning is correct?

A Dean only

B Braiden only

C Both Dean and Braiden

D Neither Dean nor Braiden

15 Keshia has to choose one shape from each box to complete a design.

Box 1	Box 2	Box 3	Box 4
square	triangle	octagon	kite
circle	hexagon	triangle	parallelogram
kite	circle	square	rectangle
decagon	rectangle	pentagon	pentagon

Which four shapes cannot be the ones Keshia chooses?

A triangle, square, kite, circle

B rectangle, pentagon, octagon, circle

C parallelogram, pentagon, triangle, octagon

D kite, rectangle, hexagon, pentagon

16 Ingrid ate 3 jellybeans one after the other. The jellybeans are either red or orange. The first one she ate was red and the last one was orange.

Which **must** be true?

A Ingrid ate an orange jellybean after a red jellybean.

B Ingrid ate one red and two orange jellybeans.

C Ingrid ate a red jellybean after an orange jellybean.

D Ingrid ate one orange and two red jellybeans.

☞ Answers and explanations on pages 118–120

17

The January 2022 eruption of the Hunga Tonga Hunga Ha'apai volcano in Tonga was a massive event. The eruption sent a huge plume of gas, steam and ash 30 kilometres into the sky and a tsunami wave across the ocean as far away as Japan. It was a massive eruption which scientists knew was coming but they had not pinpointed exactly when. It was fortunate the death toll from the eruption was not higher.

Which of these statements is the main idea in the text?

A The eruption of the Hunga Tonga Hunga Ha'apai volcano sent a huge plume of gas, steam and ash 30 kilometres into the sky.

B The January 2022 eruption of the Hunga Tonga Hunga Ha'apai volcano in Tonga was a massive event.

C It was fortunate the death toll from the 2022 eruption was not higher.

D The volcanic eruption of the Hunga Tonga Hunga Ha'apai in 2014 created a new island 120 metres high and two kilometres long.

18

Marty, Scarlet, Niklas and Seiya take turns to travel by bus to other schools as reserves for the debating team. Marty is recovering from the flu and has lost his voice. Their teacher has told them that if Marty can't be a reserve on Friday, then Scarlet will be one of the reserves. If Marty can be a reserve, then Niklas will go on the bus instead of Seiya.

If Scarlet is not one of the reserves on Friday, which of the other reserves will be on the bus?

A Marty only

B Seiya only

C Marty and Niklas

D Niklas and Seiya

19 A woman has four grandchildren (Charlie, Ezekiel, Ivy and Lola) and keeps photos of them on display. Every row, every column and both diagonals of a display frame have 4 photos, one of each grandchild. There is a photo of Charlie in P4, a photo of Ezekiel in S4 and a photo of Ivy in R3.

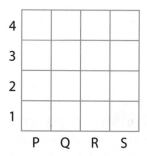

Whose photo is in Q1?

A Charlie   B Ezekiel

C Ivy   D Lola

☞ **Answers and explanations on pages 118–120**

SAMPLE TEST

20

A beehive is a very busy place, more like a city than a home. The hive has only one queen bee. But it has several hundred drone bees—and up to 50 000 worker bees. The worker bees have different jobs. These include:

- building new cells to add to the honeycomb
- cleaning the hive
- guarding the hive
- feeding the queen and the larvae
- leaving the hive to collect nectar from flowers.

This is why people say a busy place is a 'hive of activity'.

Which of the following statements best expresses the main idea of the text?

A Worker bees have different jobs.

B Beehives are very busy.

C A beehive has only one queen bee.

D People use different expressions to describe busy places.

☞ **Answers and explanations on pages 118–120**

SAMPLE TEST

25 MIN

1 Sally's mother gave her $20 to spend at the school fair. She spent $4.50 on rides, $5.55 on food and $6.00 at the sideshows. How much did she have left?

A $3.95   B $4.95
C $4.05   D $3.05
E $4.85

2 Two of these shapes are the same except that one of the two has been rotated half a turn (180°).

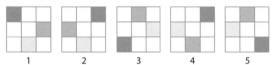

1   2   3   4   5

Which two?

A 1 and 3
B 2 and 3
C 3 and 4
D 1 and 5
E 4 and 5

3 What number is eight hundreds more than 37 519?

A 37 599
B 45 519
C 38 319
D 36 719
E 38 219

4 Which of these rectangles has $\frac{3}{4}$ shaded?

X   Y   Z

A X only
B Y only
C Z only
D Y and Z only
E X, Y and Z

5 The grid is divided into squares of side length 10 m.

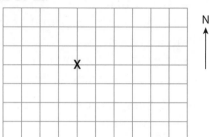

Ed begins at point X. He walks 20 m north, then 30 m east, 50 m south, 40 m west and 30 m north. How far is Ed from his starting point?

A 10 m   B 30 m
C 70 m   D 110 m
E 170 m

6 One half of a design has been completed. The dashed line will be a line of symmetry in the finished design.

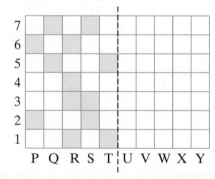

Which of these squares will **not** be shaded?

A U1   B V4   C W3   D X5   E Y6

7 Pat got on a bus at 11:25 am. He got off the bus at twenty minutes to one in the afternoon. How long was Pat on the bus?

A 1 hour 15 minutes
B 45 minutes
C 1 hour 45 minutes
D 55 minutes
E 2 hours 15 minutes

☞ **Answers and explanations on pages 120–121**

SAMPLE TEST

8 Jess has painted three of the palings in this fence.

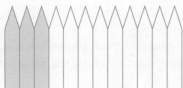

How many more palings does she need to paint so that three-quarters of the fence is painted?

A 7   B 6   C 5   D 4   E 3

9 Together Ayesha and Jake found 36 shells at the beach. Ayesha found twice as many as Jake. **How many** shells did Ayesha find?

A 9   B 12   C 18   D 24   E 27

10 Modena works part-time at a shop. She works from 9:00 am until 12 noon on Mondays, Wednesdays and Fridays and from 12 noon until 4:00 pm on Tuesdays and Thursdays. Which of these expressions could be used to find the number of hours she works each week?

A $2 \times (3 + 4)$ B $2 \times 3 + 3 \times 4$
C $3 \times 3 + 2 \times 4$ D $3 \times (2 + 4)$
E $3 \times (3 + 4)$

11 ♦ represents a number.

$$58 + ♦ = 94 - 17$$

What number does ♦ represent?

A 17   B 19   C 41   D 53   E 135

12 Two jugs hold juice as shown.

The smaller jug holds two litres of juice when full. Juice is poured from the larger jug into the smaller jug until it is full. **How much** juice will be left in the larger jug?

A 1 L   B 1.5 L
C 2 L   D 2.5 L
E 3 L

13 Nigel wants to buy 10 bread rolls. The rolls can be bought for 40 cents each or packets of 6 cost $2.00. What is the lowest price Nigel can pay?

A $2.40   B $3.00
C $3.40   D $3.60
E $4.00

14 Cody takes 7 identical cubes and glues them together in a line.

He picks up his set of cubes and looks at it from every direction. **How many faces** of the cubes can he see?

A 36   B 30   C 28   D 24   E 22

15 James spins this spinner.

Which of the following statements is/are **correct**?

1 James is equally likely to spin a 2 or a 3.
2 James is more likely to spin a number greater than 3 than a number less than 3.
3 James is equally likely to spin an odd number or an even number.

A 1 only   B 1 or 2 only
C 1 or 3 only   D 2 or 3 only
E 1, 2 or 3

☞ Answers and explanations on pages 120–121

16 Megan has this square.

She cuts the square into two pieces with one straight-line cut. One of the pieces is a triangle. Which of these could be the **other piece**?

  X   triangle
  Y   quadrilateral
  Z   pentagon

A X only   B Y only
C X and Y only   D X and Z only
E X, Y or Z

17 These are the first five terms of a sequence:
        2,   5,   8,   11,   14 …
What is the **sum** of the 7th and 10th terms?

A 17   B 19   C 43   D 49   E 52

18 Some families were asked how many children they had. The results are shown in the graph.

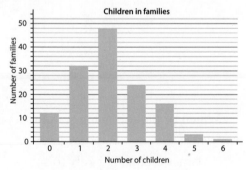

Which statements are **correct**?

  X   More families had 5 or 6 children than had none.

  Y   More than 100 families had 1, 2 or 3 children.

  Z   Exactly three times as many families had 2 children as had 4 children.

A X only   B Y only
C Z only   D X or Y only
E Y or Z only

19 A grid has been drawn on a field and X has been used to mark the positions of some players.

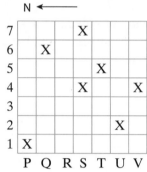

Zak is standing at S4. Haseeb is somewhere south-east of Zak. Where might **Haseeb be standing**?

A P1   B Q6   C T5   D U2   E V4

20 Billy made this shape from 10 squares each 1 cm long and 1 cm wide.

He then adds 2 more squares (again each 1 cm long and 1 cm wide) and the perimeter of his shape is increased by 4 cm. Which of these could be Billy's new shape?

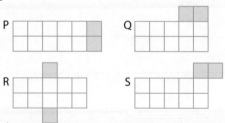

A P only   B Q only
C R only   D Both P and Q
E Both R and S

☞ **Answers and explanations on pages 120–121**

Analysing the purpose of parts of a text

ACTIVITY: You need to identify the main reason(s) the author has for writing the text and to work out how its parts relate to that purpose. Each part of the text will connect with that purpose in a particular way.

Read the text below then answer the question.

How the Whale Got his Throat

In the sea, once upon a time, O my Best Beloved, there was a Whale, and he ate fishes. He ate the starfish and the garfish, and the crab and the dab, and the plaice and the dace, and the skate and his mate, and the mackereel and the pickereel, and the really truly twirly-whirly eel. All the fishes he could find in all the sea he ate with his mouth—so! Till at last there was only one small fish left in all the sea, and he was a small Astute Fish, and he swam a little behind the Whale's right ear, so as to be out of harm's way. Then the Whale stood up on his tail and said, 'I'm hungry.' And the small Astute Fish said in a small astute voice, 'Noble and generous Cetacean, have you ever tasted Man?'

'No,' said the Whale. 'What is it like?'

'Nice,' said the small Astute Fish. 'Nice but nubbly.'

'Then fetch me some,' said the Whale, and he made the sea froth up with his tail.

'One at a time is enough,' said the Astute Fish. 'If you swim to latitude Fifty North, longitude Forty West (that is magic), you will find, sitting *on* a raft, *in* the middle of the sea, with nothing on but a pair of blue canvas breeches, a pair of suspenders (you must *not* forget the suspenders, Best Beloved), and a jack-knife, one ship-wrecked Mariner, who, it is only fair to tell you, is a man of infinite-resource-and-sagacity.'

From 'How the Whale Got his Throat' in *Just So Stories* by Rudyard Kipling

Analysing the purpose of parts of a text

SAMPLE QUESTION

The narrator includes a list of sea creatures to

A teach the reader the names of all the creatures in the sea.

B suggest how greedy the Whale is.

C demonstrate the narrator's expertise.

D explain how much he likes fish.

STRATEGY

Think about whether the part of the text in the question is there to entertain, inform or persuade, or for some combination of these. Look at the kind of language used and think about the relationship of the text you are asked to comment on and its relationship to the whole of the text.

The narrator provides an unusually long list of the names of sea creatures eaten by the Whale. He reels off their names in rhyming pairs and by using a sing-song rhythm—almost as if he is playing a game. This creates the sense that the list of fish the Whale eats could go on forever. You can work out the purpose is to list the fish in an amusing way but also to give information about the Whale's extraordinary appetite.

Now look at options **A–D** and decide which best answers the question.

B is correct. The list implies the whale doesn't discriminate or choose what he will eat but eats everything in his environment. Even then he is still hungry! He has a bottomless appetite.

The other options are incorrect. The list is neither there to educate the reader about the names of fish, nor so the author can show off how many names of fish he knows, nor to explain his own feelings about fish. He has a more important purpose in wanting to show the greediness of the whale.

Making a judgement about a character and their relationship with another character

ACTIVITY: You need to look at what each character says and does, and work out how the situation they are in affects how they act towards each other.

Read the text below then answer the question.

How the Whale Got his Throat

In the sea, once upon a time, O my Best Beloved, there was a Whale, and he ate fishes. He ate the starfish and the garfish, and the crab and the dab, and the plaice and the dace, and the skate and his mate, and the mackereel and the pickereel, and the really truly twirly-whirly eel. All the fishes he could find in all the sea he ate with his mouth—so! Till at last there was only one small fish left in all the sea, and he was a small Astute Fish, and he swam a little behind the Whale's right ear, so as to be out of harm's way. Then the Whale stood up on his tail and said, 'I'm hungry.' And the small Astute Fish said in a small astute voice, 'Noble and generous Cetacean, have you ever tasted Man?'

'No,' said the Whale. 'What is it like?'

'Nice,' said the small Astute Fish. 'Nice but nubbly.'

'Then fetch me some,' said the Whale, and he made the sea froth up with his tail.

'One at a time is enough,' said the Astute Fish. 'If you swim to latitude Fifty North, longitude Forty West (that is magic), you will find, sitting *on* a raft, *in* the middle of the sea, with nothing on but a pair of blue canvas breeches, a pair of suspenders (you must *not* forget the suspenders, Best Beloved), and a jack-knife, one ship-wrecked Mariner, who, it is only fair to tell you, is a man of infinite-resource-and-sagacity.'

From 'How the Whale Got his Throat' in *Just So Stories* by Rudyard Kipling

Making a judgement about a character and their relationship with another character

SAMPLE QUESTION

The Astute Fish calls the Whale 'Noble and generous Cetacean' because he

A is very impressed by the Whale.

B is terrified the whale will eat him.

C wants to flatter the Whale.

D always refers to other sea creatures in this way.

STRATEGY

You are being asked to make a judgement about a character and his relationship with another character. You need to make a judgement based on evidence about what the character does and says in the text and how the character interacts with or relates to others. Think about the particular situation the characters are in and how this might affect their behaviour.

You know the Whale is dangerous and a predator of fish. You know the Acute Fish is clever because he is the only fish in the sea able to outwit the Whale and save himself from being eaten. When the Acute Fish addresses the Whale as 'Noble and generous Cetacean', you doubt the sincerity of his words as there is no reason for him to think the Whale has either of these qualities. He must have a plan in mind to get the Whale to do what he wants, even though we can't tell what the plan is at this stage.

Now look at the options **A–D** and decide which best answers the question.

C is correct. The Astute Fish is, as his name implies, a very clever fish. You can work out that the Astute Fish knows the most likely way to get the Whale to do what he wants is to flatter him by calling him names that make him sound important.

A is incorrect. While the Astute Fish is well aware the Whale is a danger to all the fish in the sea, he is not impressed by his greed and thinks he can outwit him.

B is incorrect. The Astute Fish knows he is cleverer than the Whale and that he can protect himself from him with his sly tricks.

D is incorrect. There is no evidence the Astute Whale uses flattering names of this kind with other sea creatures.

PRACTICE QUESTIONS

Read the text below then answer the questions.

How the Whale Got his Throat

In the sea, once upon a time, O my Best Beloved, there was a Whale, and he ate fishes. He ate the starfish and the garfish, and the crab and the dab, and the plaice and the dace, and the skate and his mate, and the mackereel and the pickereel, and the really truly twirly-whirly eel. All the fishes he could find in all the sea he ate with his mouth—so! Till at last there was only one small fish left in all the sea, and he was a small Astute Fish, and he swam a little behind the Whale's right ear, so as to be out of harm's way. Then the Whale stood up on his tail and said, 'I'm hungry.' And the small Astute Fish said in a small astute voice, 'Noble and generous Cetacean, have you ever tasted Man?'

'No,' said the Whale. 'What is it like?'

'Nice,' said the small Astute Fish. 'Nice but nubbly.'

'Then fetch me some,' said the Whale, and he made the sea froth up with his tail.

'One at a time is enough,' said the Astute Fish. 'If you swim to latitude Fifty North, longitude Forty West (that is magic), you will find, sitting *on* a raft, *in* the middle of the sea, with nothing on but a pair of blue canvas breeches, a pair of suspenders (you must *not* forget the suspenders, Best Beloved), and a jack-knife, one ship-wrecked Mariner, who, it is only fair to tell you, is a man of infinite-resource-and-sagacity.'

From 'How the Whale Got his Throat' in *Just So Stories* by Rudyard Kipling

1　The Astute Fish includes details of latitude and longitude to

   A　make sure the Whale swims to the wrong place.

   B　persuade the Whale it is an easy swim.

   C　baffle the Whale.

   D　make sure the Whale swims to the right place.

2　How does the Astute Fish first catch the attention of the Whale?

   A　with flattery

   B　by promising it food

   C　by swimming out of its sight

   D　by being sympathetic

☞ **Answers and explanations on page 122**

Making a judgement about the author's values and attitudes

ACTIVITY: You have to work out what the author's values (standards of behaviour) and attitudes (opinions or feelings) are towards the subject of the text. This will be evident in the tone used by the author (scornful, approving, etc.).

Read the extract from the poem below by DH Lawrence then answer the question.

Baby Tortoise

You know what it is to be born alone,
   Baby tortoise!

The first day to heave your feet little by little
   from the shell,
Not yet awake,
And remain lapsed on earth,
Not quite alive.

A tiny, fragile, half-animate bean.

To open your tiny beak-mouth, that looks as if
   it would never open,
Like some iron door;

To lift the upper hawk-beak from the
   lower base
And reach your skinny little neck
And take your first bite at some dim bit
   of herbage,
Alone, small insect,
Tiny bright-eye,
Slow one.

To take your first solitary bite
And move on your slow, solitary hunt.
Your bright, dark little eye,
Your eye of a dark disturbed night,
Under its slow lid, tiny baby tortoise,
So indomitable.

SAMPLE QUESTION

The poet's attitude to the tortoise is

A critical.

B anxious.

C admiring.

D affectionate.

STRATEGY

You are being asked to make a judgement about the author's attitude to the subject of the poem.

You need to work out the tone the poet uses to identify his attitude towards his subject. What words does he choose to describe his subject and its behaviour? What do these words suggest about his attitude to it? How does he describe his subject's interaction with the world he is born into?

The poet observes every aspect of the tortoise's struggle: how his body works, what he does, what he is up against and what he achieves. The words chosen to describe the tortoise's movements reveal how difficult these struggles are for him.

For example, opening its mouth for the first time is like forcing open doors that are firmly shut: 'To open your tiny beak-mouth, that looks as if it would / never open, / Like some iron door'. Yet the tortoise doesn't give up and continues to make his way into the world.

Now look at the options **A–D** and decide which best answers the question.

C is correct. The poet stresses how tiny the tortoise is and the difficulty of the tasks he has to undertake in order to survive. He admires the way the tortoise's spirit is not defeated by these struggles as he presses on against all odds.

A and B are incorrect. The poet does not express criticism of or anxiety about the tortoise.

D is incorrect. Although there may be a note of affection in his attitude to the baby tortoise, it is mainly admiration for the way it behaves that is expressed.

Identifying the meaning of a word in context

ACTIVITY: You have to work out what the context is and how it gives meaning to the word. The context is everything that influences, acts upon or is connected with the word in the text.

Read the extract from the poem below by DH Lawrence then answer the question.

Baby Tortoise

You know what it is to be born alone,
    Baby tortoise!

The first day to heave your feet little by little
    from the shell,
Not yet awake,
And remain lapsed on earth,
Not quite alive.

A tiny, fragile, half-animate bean.

To open your tiny beak-mouth, that looks as if
    it would never open,
Like some iron door;

To lift the upper hawk-beak from the
    lower base
And reach your skinny little neck
And take your first bite at some dim bit
    of herbage,
Alone, small insect,
Tiny bright-eye,
Slow one.

To take your first solitary bite
And move on your slow, solitary hunt.
Your bright, dark little eye,
Your eye of a dark disturbed night,
Under its slow lid, tiny baby tortoise,
So indomitable.

SAMPLE QUESTION

What is the meaning of the word 'indomitable' in the last line of the poem?

A busily going about his activities

B lively and energetic

C able to see in the dark

D unable to be defeated

STRATEGY

You are being asked to identify the meaning of a word in its context. Words can change their meanings in different contexts so it is essential to think about the context: where the word occurs and how it fits in. You may know that *in* as a prefix often means 'not'; this may help you work out the meaning of the word.

You can work out that the poet is describing the many difficulties the baby tortoise faces and how he deals with each of these. His small size and his being without any help are emphasised. As he

manages to overcome each difficulty, his achievements begin to seem quite heroic. The poem builds to the final exclamation of the stanza: 'So indomitable'. These words sum up what the poet feels is so special about the tortoise. Nothing seems able to crush his spirit!

Now look at the options **A–D** and decide which best answers the question.

D is correct. It is the tortoise's willingness to continue to overcome the challenges he faces through each step of his existence that makes the poet exclaim 'So indomitable'.

A and B are incorrect. The tortoise does not go 'busily' about his activities and is not lively.

C is incorrect. Although the poet refers to the tortoise's efforts to see, this is just one of his many achievements. The words 'So indomitable' sums up the nature of all the achievements that make the baby tortoise so special.

Read the extract from the poem by Henry Lawson below then answer the questions.

Andy's Gone With Cattle

Our Andy's gone with cattle now—
Our hearts are out of order—
With drought he's gone to battle now
Across the Queensland border.

He's left us in dejection now;
Our thoughts with him are roving;
It's dull on this selection* now,
Since Andy went a-droving.

Who now shall wear the cheerful face
In times when things are slackest?
And who shall whistle round the place
When Fortune frowns her blackest?

*property

1 How does the narrator feel toward Andy, the drover?

   A The narrator despises him.

   B The narrator admires him.

   C The narrator is critical of him.

   D The narrator approves of him.

2 What is the meaning of 'out of order' in the first stanza?

   A requiring medical attention

   B out of sorts

   C full of misery

   D broken

☞ **Answers and explanations on page 122**

Identifying how information and ideas are sequenced

ACTIVITY

Sequencing involves putting ideas and information in a logical order. To work out how sentences are connected to each other within a text you need to consider what goes before and after, and how it fits into the whole text.

SAMPLE QUESTIONS

Read the text below then answer the questions.

Three sentences have been removed from the text. Choose from the sentences (**A–D**) the one which fits each gap (**1–3**). There is one extra sentence which you do not need to use.

The Noongar Language

Noongar is the language spoken in the Noongar nation, which covers the entire south-west corner of Western Australia. **1** _____ Currently only a small number of Noongar peoples are left who still speak the language fluently, although thousands still use some of its phrases, words and greetings.

The Noongar Language Centre was established to ensure the Noongar language would be preserved for future generations. **2** _____ It is time-consuming work but the Centre is encouraged by the excellent progress being made and can report the language is now in rapid recovery.

A recent event likely to further help in the recovery of this language is the making of a new version of an old film, *Fist of Fury*. **3** _____ It was made through a collaboration between the First Nations production company Boomerang and Spear and the Perth Festival.

The Centre has an online shop where you can purchase posters, plaques for different clans, beautifully illustrated Dreaming stories such as Koorlbardi wer Waardong (The Magpie and the Crow), among other goods and publications.

Identifying how information and ideas are sequenced

A   In order to achieve this purpose they have worked hard at making recordings, building dictionaries, grammars and books, and providing language learning courses.

B   The remake of the film is performed by Noongar peoples and dubbed with the Noongar language.

C   'Kaya' means hello in the Noongar language.

D   It has been spoken by First Nations Australians for many thousands of years.

STRATEGY

Read the whole text first so you know what it is about. Then read the missing sentences and find the first space, numbered 1. Think about the subject of its paragraph. Look closely at the sentences before and after the space and work out the sequence of ideas and information. Repeat this procedure for questions 2 and 3.

You need to select the sentence from **A–D** that best connects with these sentences.

1 **D is correct.** In the opening sentence the author gives information about the Noongar language and tells where it is spoken in Australia. This sentence adds the information that the Noongar language has been spoken by First Nations people for a very long time.
The sentence that follows explains that today there are only a small number of people who still speak this language.

2 **A is correct.** In the previous sentence the purpose of setting up the Noongar Language Centre is explained. This sentence outlines the many different resources the Centre has built up to achieve this purpose. The sentence that follows adds a comment about the difficulties of the Centre's task and the excellent progress they have made.

3 **B is correct.** In the previous sentence the author refers to the making of a recent film that may contribute to the recovery of the Noongar language. This sentence explains why this is so: it was performed by Noongar people and dubbed in their language. The sentence that follows tells who collaborated in the making of the film.

The unused sentence is C.

PRACTICE QUESTIONS

Read the text below then answer the questions.

Three sentences have been removed from the text. Choose from the sentences (**A–D**) the one which fits each gap (**1–3**). There is one extra sentence which you do not need to use.

Vale Street, Bristol, England

What makes this street, in the area known as Totterdown, so special? **1** _____ Climbing from the bottom to the top along the stepped pathway is a test of strength and fitness.

Can you guess how people park their cars in this street? **2** _____ If they forget to do this, they can be in trouble because sometimes when its icy, the cars are in danger of rolling downhill. Cyclists and skateboarders find it a very tempting sight from the top and an exciting challenge from the bottom.

At Easter time, Vale Street is closed off to traffic. The residents meet at the top of the steep hill with their boiled eggs and the owner of the egg that rolls furthest down the hill is the winner. **3** _____ But the Easter competition with boiled eggs of Vale Street, Totterdown is unique.

A They park them perpendicular to the road.

B The name Totterdown is very well chosen!

C It is thought to be the steepest street in England.

D There are equally steep streets in other parts of the world such as Wales, New Zealand and Pennsylvania.

☞ **Answers and explanations on page 122**

Comparing aspects of texts such as forms, structures, ideas and language use

ACTIVITY

You need to understand what each text is about and how it is written. This will enable you to compare the texts so you can choose the one that best provides the answer to the question.

SAMPLE QUESTIONS

Read the two texts below on the theme of biography.

For questions **1–3**, choose the option (**A** or **B**) which you think best answers the question.

Which text ...

is about someone who probably had many grandchildren? | 1 | _____

refers to someone involved in events on the world stage? | 2 | _____

suggests patience can be a virtue? | 3 | _____

TEXT A

John Parkes was born in 1766 in Halesowen, Worcester, England. He could not read or write and from the age of five or six was brought up as a nailor (a worker who forged nails) where he learned to pump the bellows on his father's forge. In 1798 he was transported as a convict on the *Barwell*. His sentence was for seven years for stealing 'a great coat, called a beaver coat, worth sixteen shillings'.

John Parkes married Margaret Southern around 1806. John and Margaret had twelve children. Initially John worked out his sentence in the Government boatyard near Circular Quay. In 1816 he was promised 50 acres in the Botany Bay District by Governor Macquarie but the grant was not finally approved until 1831.

At that time, he selected his 50 acres at the top of a ridge where the area was said to be resplendent with ironbanks, red mahogony trees, casuarinas, ferns, flannel flowers and gymea lilies. The area became commonly known as Parkes' Camp, the headquarters of a group of sawyers. John made a success of Parkes' Camp and in 1988 his achievements were recognised by a memorial erected at Earlwood Oval, NSW.

TEXT B

In 1908, when Pu Yi was not quite three, he learned he was the new Emperor of China. Pu Yi's mother fainted from shock when she heard the news! The previous Emperor had died leaving no children of his own. The Empress Dowager chose Pu Yi, from her many nephews, to take his place. She hoped he would be a puppet Emperor for her.

Comparing aspects of texts such as forms, structures, ideas and language use

Pu Yi was taken immediately to live in the imperial palace in the Forbidden City. He 'reigned' for three years but in 1912 the revolution in China forced him to leave his position. The Qing dynasty that had ruled China since 1644 was overthrown so Pu Yi was its last Emperor.

Pi Yu eventually moved to Japan where he was made Emperor of Manchuria. In 1945 he was taken prisoner by the Russians and sent back to China where he was tried as a war criminal. After he was pardoned, he lived the rest of his life in Beijing. He married several times but died without having any children. He published his autobiography, *From Emperor to Citizen*, in 1960 and this was used as the basis for a film, *The Last Emperor*, which won nine Academy Awards.

STRATEGY

When finding which text offers the answer to a question, you need to have a good grasp of what each text is about and how it is written.

TEXT A: John Parkes, a convict, is the subject of this text. His early life suggests he came from a poor, hardworking family. That he stole a coat in later life suggests he was probably still poor and in need. The events which follow suggest he turned his life around after coming to Australia where he built a new family and his good deeds were recognised by his community.

TEXT B: Pu Yi, the last Emperor of China, led a very unusual life. He was in the public eye from when he was not even three and throughout most of his life. He was caught up in world affairs probably against his will. The world learned more about how he saw his life from the autobiography he wrote, which was also made into a film.

Now look at the questions and decide which text best answers each one.

1   A is correct. You can work out that John Parkes was the father of twelve children so is likely to have had many grandchildren.

   B is incorrect. Pu Yi did not have any children of his own so could not have had any grandchildren.

2   B is correct. Pu Yi was involved in the downfall of the Chinese Empire, acting as the Emperor of Manchuria and being imprisoned and named as a war criminal in World War II.

   A is incorrect. While John Parkes was involved in the British transportation of convicts, he was not involved in any other events of world significance.

3   A is correct. John Parkes transformed his life from someone looked down on as a convict to someone highly commended by his community. He achieved this through patience (he had to wait 15 years for the land he had been promised) as well as hard work, which suggests patience can be a virtue.

   B is incorrect. The account of Pu Yi's life does not imply that patience played any significant part.

PRACTICE QUESTIONS

Read the two texts below on the theme of biography.

For questions **1–3**, choose the option (**A** or **B**) which you think best answers the question.
Which text ...

describes a family man?

1 _____

refers to a person who earns the respect of his local community?

2 _____

describes a person likely to be well educated?

3 _____

TEXT A

John Parkes was born in 1766 in Halesowen, Worcester, England. He could not read or write and from the age of five or six was brought up as a nailor (a worker who forged nails) where he learned to pump the bellows on his father's forge. In 1798 he was transported as a convict on the *Barwell*. His sentence was for seven years for stealing 'a great coat, called a beaver coat, worth sixteen shillings'.

John Parkes married Margaret Southern around 1806. John and Margaret had twelve children. Initially John worked out his sentence in the Government boatyard near Circular Quay. In 1816 he was promised 50 acres in the Botany Bay District by Governor Macquarie but the grant was not finally approved until 1831.

At that time, he selected his 50 acres at the top of a ridge where the area was said to be resplendent with ironbanks, red mahogony trees, casuarinas, ferns, flannel flowers and gymea lilies. The area became commonly known as Parkes' Camp, the headquarters of a group of sawyers. John made a success of Parkes' Camp and in 1988 his achievements were recognised by a memorial erected at Earlwood Oval, NSW.

TEXT B

In 1908, when Pu Yi was not quite three, he learned he was the new Emperor of China. Pu Yi's mother fainted from shock when she heard the news! The previous Emperor had died leaving no children of his own. The Empress Dowager chose Pu Yi, from her many nephews, to take his place. She hoped he would be a puppet Emperor for her.

Pu Yi was taken immediately to live in the imperial palace in the Forbidden City. He 'reigned' for three years but in 1912 the revolution in China forced him to leave his position. The Qing dynasty that had ruled China since 1644 was overthrown so Pu Yi was its last Emperor.

Pi Yu eventually moved to Japan where he was made Emperor of Manchuria. In 1945 he was taken prisoner by the Russians and sent back to China where he was tried as a war criminal. After he was pardoned, he lived the rest of his life in Beijing. He married several times but died without having any children. He published his autobiography, *From Emperor to Citizen*, in 1960 and this was used as the basis for a film, *The Last Emperor*, which won nine Academy Awards.

☞ **Answers and explanations on pages 122–123**

Drawing a conclusion

ACTIVITY: You need to evaluate the evidence presented in an argument. A correct conclusion must be supported by evidence. A conclusion is not possible or cannot be true if the evidence does not support it.

SAMPLE QUESTION 1

Alice was deciding what snack to take on a bushwalk.

Alice: 'I'd like some trail mix. But if I can't take trail mix, then I'll take fruitcake. And if I do take trail mix, then I'll take an orange instead of an apple.'

If Alice doesn't take fruitcake, what snack will she take on the bushwalk?

A trail mix and an orange

B an orange and an apple

C trail mix only

D an apple only

STRATEGY

1 Read the information in the box.

2 Read the question. You need to work out what Alice took on the bushwalk if she didn't take fruitcake.

3 To answer this question you need to draw a conclusion that is not stated in the text but can be worked out from the information provided.

4 There are four snacks mentioned (trail mix, fruitcake, orange and apple). From what Alice says you can conclude she will take trail mix **and** an orange (rather than an apple) or fruitcake **and** an apple (rather than an orange).

5 The question asks what she will take if she doesn't take fruitcake. Use a process of elimination to work out the answer.

A is correct. If Alice doesn't take fruitcake, you can conclude she must take trail mix. Since she takes trail mix, she must also take an orange.

B is incorrect. Alice says she will take an orange or an apple, not both.

C is incorrect. Alice says if she takes trail mix, she will take an orange as well.

D is incorrect. If Alice takes an apple, you can conclude she will also take fruitcake.

Drawing a conclusion

SAMPLE QUESTION 2

When Mo was learning to sail, his instructor told him: 'To have even a chance of being certified, you must complete ten full days of sailing and pass the written exam.'

If Mo's instructor is correct, which one of these statements must be true?

A All the sailors who have completed ten full days of sailing and passed the written exam will be certified.

B Some of the sailors who have not completed ten full days of sailing might be certified.

C None of the sailors who have not completed ten full days of sailing will be certified.

D All the sailors who pass the written exam will be certified.

STRATEGY

1 Read the information in the box.

2 Read the question. You have to work out which statement must be true.

3 To answer this question you need to draw a conclusion not stated in the text but which can be worked out from the information provided.

4 Read each statement in turn and evaluate if it can be concluded from the information provided and therefore must be true. Quickly eliminate any answers that are definitely wrong.

C is correct. According to the instructor if a sailor has not completed ten full days of sailing, they don't have a chance of being certified. Therefore none of the sailors who have not completed ten full days of sailing will be certified. So this statement must be true.

A is incorrect. According to the instructor if a sailor has not completed ten full days of sailing and passed the written exam, they **don't have a chance** of being certified. However, the instructor doesn't say completing these minimum requirements guarantees the sailor **will** be certified. So you cannot conclude with certainty that this statement is true.

B is incorrect. The instructor says a sailor **must** complete ten full days of sailing to have even a chance of being certified.

D is incorrect. A sailor who passes the written exam might not have completed the required ten full days of sailing and so might not be certified.

Identifying an assumption

ACTIVITY: You need to evaluate evidence and the conclusion drawn from that evidence to work out any assumptions made in reaching this conclusion. Note that it is easy to make assumptions that lead to incorrect conclusions.

SAMPLE QUESTION 1

Leon is walking to school carrying a saxophone case when he meets his friend Mia.

Mia: 'I didn't know you played the saxophone!'

Leon: 'I don't! This is Sam's saxophone. He left it at my house last night.'

Which assumption has Mia made in order to draw her conclusion?

A The band needs more saxophone players.

B The saxophone case belongs to Leon.

C The saxophone case belongs to Sam.

D Leon plays the saxophone.

STRATEGY

Read the information in the box.

Read the question: Which assumption has Mia made in order to draw her conclusion?

1 To answer this question you need to identify an assumption that has been made in order to draw a conclusion.

2 An assumption is not stated in a text. Instead it is something that is taken for granted.

3 First ask yourself what Mia's **conclusion** is. What is the main point she is trying to get you to accept? (Leon plays the saxophone.)

4 Now ask yourself what **evidence** she has based this conclusion on. (Leon is carrying a saxophone case.)

5 Read and think about each statement listed. Which one of these statements would you

need to **take for granted** in order to draw the conclusion Mia drew?

B is correct. For Mia's conclusion to hold it must be assumed the saxophone case belongs to Leon. (Leon is carrying a saxophone case + the saxophone case belongs to Leon means Leon plays the saxophone.)

A is incorrect. This assumption does not support Mia's conclusion that Leon plays the saxophone. (Leon is carrying a saxophone case + the band needs more saxophone players does not mean Leon plays the saxophone.)

C is incorrect. This is the real reason why Leon is carrying the saxophone case, not the assumption Mia has made.

D is incorrect. This is the conclusion Mia has drawn, based on her assumption that the saxophone case belonged to Leon.

Identifying an assumption

SAMPLE QUESTION 2

Just before Christmas the toy store displayed an advertisement in its window:

BRAND NEW AND IN STORE NOW

**The latest model Zoom-Zoom
radio-controlled car**

Every child will want one for Christmas

Which assumption has the writer of the advertisement made in order to draw a conclusion?

A The new Zoom-Zoom radio-controlled car is in store now.

B The toy store wants to sell lots of Zoom-Zoom cars.

C Every child will want a Zoom-Zoom car for Christmas.

D All children like radio-controlled cars.

STRATEGY

1 Read the information in the box.

2 Read the question. What assumption has the writer made in order to draw the conclusion in the advertisement?

3 To answer this question you need to identify an assumption that has been made in order to draw a conclusion. An assumption is not stated in a text. Instead it is something that is taken for granted.

4 First ask yourself what the writer of the advertisement's **conclusion** is. What is the main point the advertisement is trying to get you to accept? (Every child will want a Zoom-Zoom car for Christmas.)

5 Now ask yourself what **evidence** the writer has based this conclusion on. (The new Zoom-Zoom radio-controlled car is in store now.)

6 Read and think about each statement listed. Which one of these statements would you need to **take for granted** in order to draw the conclusion that the advertisement writer drew?

D is correct. For the conclusion to hold it must be assumed that all children like radio-controlled cars. (The new Zoom-Zoom radio-controlled car is in store now + all children like radio-controlled cars means every child will want a Zoom-Zoom for Christmas.)

A is incorrect. This is the evidence the writer used to support the conclusion.

B is incorrect. This is the purpose of the advertisement.

C is incorrect. This is the conclusion the writer drew, based on the assumption that all children like radio-controlled cars.

Assessing the impact of additional evidence

ACTIVITY: You need to evaluate a claim or argument and judge whether additional evidence will weaken or strengthen that argument.

SAMPLE QUESTION 1

The local council wants to plant jacaranda trees along both sides of the main street of town. The council claims that people love the purple flowers of the trees so planting them will attract tourists to the town. Some residents are fighting the plan. They say the town should plant native trees instead.

Which one of the statements below, if true, best supports the local council's claim?

A   Jacaranda trees flower for only one month of the year.

B   People take cruises to see the jacarandas around Sydney Harbour.

C   When jacaranda flowers drop they create a slipping hazard on footpaths.

D   Jacaranda trees are native to South America.

STRATEGY

1   Read the text.

2   Read the question. The question wants you to identify which statement best supports the local council's claim.

3   Clarify the claim the council is making: planting jacaranda trees will attract tourists to the town. The council supports its claim by stating that people love the purple flowers of the trees.

4   Consider the answer options. Any statement about people liking to see jacaranda trees will support the claim.

5   Judge which answer is correct. Try to quickly eliminate answers that are definitely incorrect or irrelevant to the argument. Check all answer options to ensure you have chosen the correct answer.

B is correct. The statement that people take cruises to see the jacaranda trees in another area supports the council's claim that jacaranda trees can be a tourist attraction.

A is incorrect. This statement could weaken the council's argument becasue tourists would only come to the town for that one month.

C is incorrect. This statement does not support the claim that the trees will attract tourists.

D is incorrect. Rather than supporting the council's claim, this statement supports the claim made by the residents fighting the council's plan.

Assessing the impact of additional evidence

SAMPLE QUESTION 2

Yifan wants to convince her parents to let her have a kitten. She tells them cats make the best pets because they do not cause any trouble.

Which one of these statements, if true, **weakens** Yifan's claim?

A Kittens are cute and easy to care for.

B Pet cats are good company and fun to play with.

C Cats often go out at night, without their owners realising, and kill native animals.

D Cuddling or patting a pet cat makes a person feel calm.

STRATEGY

1 Read the text.

2 Read the question. The question asks you to identify which statement **weakens** Yifan's claim.

3 Think about what Yifan claims: that cats make the best pets. She supports this claim by stating that cats do not cause any trouble.

4 Consider the answer options. Any statement that contradicts or undermines Yifan's claim will weaken it.

5 Judge which answer weakens Yifan's argument. Try to quickly eliminate answers that are definitely incorrect or irrelevant. Check all answer options to ensure you have chosen the correct answer.

C is correct. The statement that cats go out at night without their owners realising and kill native animals weakens the argument that cats do not cause any trouble.

A is incorrect. The statement that cats are easy to care for strengthens the argument that cats do not cause any trouble.

B is incorrect. The statement that cats are good company and fun strengthens the argument that cats do not cause any trouble.

D is incorrect. The statement that cuddling or patting a cat makes a person feel calm strengthens the argument that cats do not cause any trouble.

Checking reasoning to detect errors

ACTIVITY

You need to analyse the reasoning used in an argument or claim. If the reasoning holds up, the claim might be accepted. If the reasoning does not make sense or is flawed, the claim or argument can be rejected.

SAMPLE QUESTION 1

A blizzard is a type of snowstorm but not all snowstorms are blizzards. A blizzard has wind speeds over 56 km/h and visibility of less than 0.4 km. The fast winds and low visibility must last for more than three hours to be classed as a blizzard.

Atiya: 'It's so windy in this snowstorm I can hardly walk. This must be a blizzard!'

Jack: 'It's been snowing for at least four hours. This must be a blizzard!'

If the information in the box is true, whose reasoning is correct?

A   Atiya only

B   Jack only

C   Both Atiya and Jack

D   Neither Atiya nor Jack

STRATEGY

1   Read the information in the box. You are given a definition of a blizzard. It is a type of snowstorm with wind speeds over 56 km/h and visibility less than 0.4 km that lasts for over three hours.

2   Read the question. Whose reasoning is correct?

3   Evaluate the statements made by Atiya and Jack and compare their statements with the information in the box. Decide whose reasoning is correct.

4   Use a process of elimination to work out your answer.

D is correct. Neither Atiya nor Jack's reasoning is correct.

A is incorrect. Atiya reasons that because the snowstorm is also very windy, it **must** be a blizzard. Her reasoning is incorrect. Atiya cannot say with certainty that it is a blizzard since she does not know if the wind speed is over 56 km/h. She also does not mention the other two requirements: low visibility and over three hours duration.

B is incorrect. Jack reasons that because it's been snowing for at least four hours it **must** be a blizzard. He is correct that the conditions must last for over three hours for a snowstorm to be called a blizzard. But his reasoning is incorrect because he doesn't mention the other two requirements: low visibility and wind speed.

C is incorrect. You can eliminate this answer because you have worked out that neither Atiya nor Jack's reasoning is correct.

Checking reasoning to detect errors

SAMPLE QUESTION 2

Mr Street said: 'To have any chance of winning a prize in our class readathon, you must read for at least 20 minutes at least five times a week.'

Kinta: 'I'll win a prize for sure! I read every night before bed for 20 minutes.'

Which one of the following statements shows the mistake Kinta has made?

A Reading for the minimum time required does not guarantee a prize in the readathon.

B Reading an exciting book before bed can keep you awake all night.

C Reading at home is not as good as reading at school.

D Completing the readathon challenge by reading on the weekend is not allowed.

STRATEGY

1 Read the information in the box.

2 Read the question. Which statement shows the mistake Kinta has made?

3 Evaluate Kinta's statement in light of the information Mr Street gives. Mr Street says that to have **any chance** of winning a prize, students **must** read for at least 20 minutes at least five times a week.

4 Judge each answer option. Try to quickly eliminate answers that are obviously incorrect.

5 Check all answer options.

A is correct. Kinta seems to read for the required time. However, he says he will win a prize for sure whereas Mr Street says that reading for the required time gives only a **chance** of winning a prize. So this option shows the mistake Kinta has made.

B is incorrect. This statement is irrelevant to winning a prize in the readathon and is not a mistake made by Kinta.

C is incorrect. Mr Street does not mention anything about reading at home or at school so this is not a mistake made by Kinta.

D is incorrect. Mr Street does not mention anything about reading on the weekend so this is not a mistake made by Kinta.

PRACTICE QUESTIONS

1

Dora, Jim and Lily each have a birthday in the next month. They are talking about the kind of party they would like to have. Dora would like a pinata, tacos, a sleepover, cake and a movie. Jim would like a disco, a movie and cake. Lily would like tacos, mini-golf, cake, laser tag and a movie.

What does Dora want that neither Jim nor Lily wants?

A tacos and pinata

B sleepover and cake

C laser tag and disco

D pinata and sleepover

2

Sam's teacher, Ms Wilson, saw Sam talking during a test. She told Sam he had to stay back at lunchtime and finish the test on his own.

Sam: 'There's nothing wrong with talking during the test. Everyone else was!'

Which assumption has Sam made in order to draw his conclusion?

A It's okay to do something if everyone else is doing it.

B There's nothing wrong with talking during a test.

C Ms Wilson likes to set tests for her class.

D Everyone in Sam's class was talking during the test.

☞ **Answers and explanations on page 123**

3

A coastal engineer says: 'The proposed extension to the seven-metre vertical sea wall at North Beach should not go ahead. The existing wall is already causing increased erosion from which the beach may never recover.'

Which one of these statements, if true, best supports the engineer's claim?

A Sloping rock walls, rather than vertical walls, have been used successfully in other areas.

B Community groups are meeting to discuss the issue.

C An environmental study shows that an extension to the vertical wall will ensure backwash and ultimately destroy the beach.

D The seawall at North Beach was built to protect the many historic houses along the coastline.

4

Mr Flint, the soccer coach, says only those players who attended every training session during the season will be allowed to play in the special exhibition match.

Ethan: 'I attended every training session during the season so I'll definitely be playing in the exhibition match.'

Sara: 'I missed a training session during the season so I won't be able to play in the exhibition match.'

If the information in the box is true, whose reasoning is correct?

A Ethan only   B Sara only

C Both Ethan and Sara

D Neither Ethan nor Sara

Working with patterns and codes

ACTIVITY

The requirement for this kind of reasoning is the ability to identify a relationship or pattern between numbers or shapes and apply the rule for that relationship to find further terms of that sequence.

Questions involving codes require understanding of how one set of symbols (letters or numbers) can represent another set (in this case, a word). The cross-use of numbers and letters can be a difficult concept at first and clear analysis of the information and question is essential. The words and numbers should be regarded merely as symbols in these questions. Looking for patterns, especially similarities, is the key. It is important to have a general strategy that is as simple as possible.

SAMPLE QUESTION 1

> In a sequence, each number is 3 less than double the previous number. Mel finds the two numbers immediately before 19 in this sequence and adds them together.

What is Mel's answer?

A 15   B 16   C 17   D 18

STRATEGY

In this question we are given the rule for the sequence but not the terms themselves. We need to apply the rule to the number we are given.

Here we are given the term 19 and need to find the terms before it so we need to work backwards. We are told that each number is 3 less than double the previous number. So 19 must be 3 less than double the term before it. 19 is 3 less than 22 so 22 is double the previous term. We know that 22 is 2 × 11 so the previous term was 11. We need to apply the same process to find the term before 11. As 11 is 3 less than 14 and 14 is 2 × 7, the number before 11 is 7.

We have found the two numbers immediately before 19 in Mel's sequence. We now need to add them together.

As 7 + 11 = 18, Mel's answer should be 18.
D is correct.

SAMPLE QUESTION 2

> A spy uses a secret code in which DARWIN is written XZMTPO.

How might the word SYDNEY be written?

A SYXNEY   B QLXOGL
C QGXOLH   D QGOXLG

STRATEGY

A pencil and paper can be used to make it clearer in your mind. Make a chart of the corresponding letters.

$$D \quad A \quad R \quad W \quad I \quad N$$
$$X \quad Z \quad M \quad T \quad P \quad O$$

Look for common letters in the two coded words, DARWIN and SYDNEY. N and D are common to both words and in the code you can see D is represented by X and N is represented by O. In SYDNEY, these are the third and fourth letters.

So the correct answer must have X and O in third and fourth positions. A quick check means we can discard A—here the X is in the right position (third) but the O is not—and D, where the O and X are the wrong way round (fourth and third instead of third and fourth). This leaves B and C.

In SYDNEY the Y appears twice so the coded word must have the same letter in positions 2 and 6. C does not fit this pattern. In B, L is repeated in the second and last positions. **B is correct.**

PRACTICE QUESTIONS

1 In the following series of shapes, which would replace the question mark?

⇦   ↖   ⇧   ↗   ⇨   ↘   ⇩   **?**

A ⇗   B ↙   C ↙   D ←

2 What is the missing number in this sequence?

1   2   4   7   **?**   16   22   29

A 9   B 10   C 11   D 12

3 What number is next in this sequence?

13   9   18   14   28   24   **?**

A 20   B 48   C 28   D 38

4 Below is a code of numbers for letters. Each number stands for one letter only. What message could it be giving?

2 6 3 7 1 6 3 7 9 6 8

A Come to Sydney

B Come back now

C Come home Joe

D Come home now

5 In a sequence, each number is 8 more than half the previous number. If the first number in the sequence is 80, what is the fifth number?

A 18   B 20   C 22   D 24

6 If the code for CAGE is 3175 and for BAG it is 217, how would HEAD be written using the same code?

A 8514   B 4158

C 4518   D 8154

7 The sentence below is encoded as the numbers written beneath each letter. Using the same method (not the same code), what would be the code for AGAINST?

H E   F L E W   T O
1 2   3 4 2 5   6 7

E N G L A N D
2 8 9 4 10 8 11

Y E S T E R D A Y
12 2 13 6 2 14 11 10 12

A 1214567   B 1213456

C 109101881314   D 1234567

8 The pattern in this diagram is 15 = 5 × 3.

The same pattern is used in this diagram but some numbers are missing and have been replaced with P, Q, R, S and T. What is S + T?

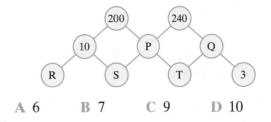

A 6   B 7   C 9   D 10

9 Maria takes a book out of the library and reads this sign: 'If a book is one day overdue, the fine is 1 cent; if it is two days overdue, the fine adds on 2c; if it is three days overdue, the fine is another 4c'. The rule is: The fine for each day increases by double the day before. If Maria's book is one week overdue, what will her fine be?

A $0.70   B $0.07   C $0.64   D $1.27

☞ Answers and explanations on pages 123–124

Logical reasoning

ACTIVITY

The requirement for this type of reasoning is the ability to think clearly and identify the key elements of the question. Work through the given information and place things in order or determine what must be true and what must be false.

SAMPLE QUESTION 1

A flag has five horizontal stripes in three different colours: red, yellow and blue. Two of the stripes are blue. The top stripe is red and the bottom stripe is blue.

Which **must** be correct?

A Two of the stripes are red.

B Two of the stripes are yellow.

C A red stripe is next to a blue stripe.

D A yellow stripe is next to a red stripe.

STRATEGY

Read the question carefully and take time to think about what is required. Here we are looking for the statement that **must** be true. This doesn't mean the other statements will necessarily be false. The flag had five horizontal stripes and the diagram helps us see that. The stripes are in three different colours and we must use our common sense to realise that adjacent stripes must be different colours. The top stripe is red so the second stripe must be either yellow or blue. If the second stripe is yellow then that stripe, a yellow stripe, is next to the top stripe, a red stripe. In this case D will be true.

If the second stripe is blue (and we know the fifth stripe is also blue), the third and fourth stripes can only be red and yellow in some order. So a yellow stripe must be next to a red stripe so D will be true. **D is correct.**

Two stripes are blue and there are three more stripes so either two are red or two are yellow. One of the statements in A and B will be true but we don't know which. Similarly a red stripe might be next to a blue stripe, making C true. However, the order could be red, yellow, blue, yellow, blue meaning a red stripe might not be next to a blue stripe and C might not be true.

SAMPLE QUESTION 2

Summer has to choose an activity to do one day each week for the next 4 weeks. The possible choices are:

Week 1	Week 2	Week 3	Week 4
Swimming	Boating	Swimming	Bushwalking
Bushwalking	Puzzles	Boating	Photography
Puzzles	Tennis	Pottery	Tennis
Reading	Dancing	Reading	Handball

Summer wants to choose swimming, bushwalking and photography. Which of these can she **not** choose?

A Pottery B Puzzles C Tennis   D Boating

STRATEGY

Summer must choose one activity from each week. None of her choices are in week 2 so her final choice must come from week 2. Pottery is not available in week 2 so this is the activity she cannot choose. **A is correct.**

PRACTICE QUESTIONS

1 Five people are lined up in a queue. Jennifer is behind Ashleigh but in front of Ezra. Ashleigh is behind Martin but in front of Kate. Who is second in the line?

A Ashleigh

B Jennifer

C Kate

D Martin

2 Four girls—Ava, Ellen, Sally and Tiffany—are sitting in a row. Sally is to the left of Ava. Ellen is to the right of Tiffany. Tiffany is to the right of Sally. Which must be correct?

A Ellen is furthest right.

B Tiffany is furthest left.

C Ava is furthest right.

D Sally is furthest left.

3 Olivia, Zeb, Tahlia and Noah are sitting at a picnic table at a park close to where a river flows into the ocean. Two people are facing the river and the other two have their back to the river. The beach is on one side and the road on the other.

Olivia is sitting next to Noah. Zeb is facing the river and Tahlia is diagonally opposite Olivia.

Which must be correct?

A Olivia is on the side next to the beach.

B Zeb is directly opposite Olivia.

C Tahlia has her back to the river.

D Noah is on the side next to the road.

4 Some boys took part in some races. Each week there was a different winner and the names of the boys who filled the top four places each week is given in the table in alphabetical order. No boys shared the same name.

Week 1	Week 2	Week 3	Week 4
Billy	Oliver	Caleb	Alex
James	Peter	Max	James
Max	Xavier	Mo	Xavier
Peter	Zac	Oliver	Zac

In week 5 the four boys who won in each of the previous weeks filled the 4 places. They included James, Mo and Oliver. Who was definitely not one of the week 5 placegetters?

A Alex

B Billy

C Caleb

D Max

5 Six women—Abigail, Dana, Jessica, Laura, Madison and Vanessa—all live in the same street in six houses all in a row.

Madison and Vanessa live furthest apart.

Exactly one woman lives between Jessica and Laura.

Dana lives next to Madison.

At least two women live between Laura and Dana.

Who lives next door to Vanessa?

A Abigail

B Dana

C Jessica

D Laura

☞ **Answers and explanations on pages 124–125**

Solving problems

ACTIVITY

When solving problems it is important to read the question carefully and understand what is required. Some questions might be quite unusual or different to what has been seen before. So take time to think!

Effective methods of solving problems include making a table or list, looking for a pattern, using trial and error, drawing a picture or graph, working backwards or solving a similar but simpler problem.

SAMPLE QUESTION 1

Levi has a set of drawers where he keeps notepads, paper, envelopes, stamps, pens, pencils, cards, clips and labels. He organised the drawers to each hold just one type of thing but forgot to label them.

Levi knows that pens, pencils and paper are all in the top row. He also knows the labels are directly above the cards, right of the notepads and left of the stamps.

```
left     | 1 | 2 | 3 |
         | 4 | 5 | 6 |  right
         | 7 | 8 | 9 |
```

Which **must** be correct?

A The pencils are in 2.

B The notepads are in 6.

C The envelopes are in 7.

D The cards are in 8.

STRATEGY

The information given in the question must be sorted through to find which one of the statements **must** be correct. This doesn't mean the other statements **cannot** be correct, just that they **might not** be correct.

Here we are told that pens, pencils and paper are all in the top row but there is no other information to tell us which of the top drawers those items are in. We know the labels are directly above the cards, which means the labels cannot be in the bottom row. As they are not in the top row either, the labels must be in the middle row. The labels are right of the notepads and left of the stamps so they must be in the middle of the middle row—in drawer 5. The notepads will be in 4 and the stamps in 6. Because the labels are directly above the cards, the cards must be in the middle of the bottom row—in drawer 8. The statement that must be correct is that the cards are in 8.

The pencils might or might not be in 2. The envelopes will be in either 7 or 9. D is correct.

Solving problems

SAMPLE QUESTION 2

> Pencils and pens are sold at a stall. Eight pencils cost a total of 40 cents and 6 pens cost a total of 90 cents.

What will 6 pencils and 8 pens cost from that stall?

A $1.20   B $1.30   C $1.40   D $1.50

STRATEGY

Read the question carefully and consider what is required. We are given the price of a certain number of items and must use that information to find the cost of a different number of items. We could use the unitary method, which simply means to first find the cost of one of each item. The working might be simpler if we make use of common multiples.

Here we know the price of 8 pencils and we want the price of 6 pencils. 8 pencils cost 40c so each pencil costs 5c (after dividing both parts by 8). So 6 pencils will cost 6 × 5c or 30c.

We also know the price of 6 pens and we want the price of 8 pens. As 2 divides into both 6 and 8, it is a common multiple. So if 6 pens cost 90c, then 2 pens will cost 30c (on dividing both parts by 3). If 2 pens cost 30c, 8 pens will cost 120c or $1.20 (after multiplying both parts by 4).

The total cost is $0.30 + $1.20 or $1.50.
D is correct.

PRACTICE QUESTIONS

1 Pippa planted 3 rose bushes in a row. The roses are either pink or white. The first one she planted was pink and the last one was white.

Which **must** be true?

A Pippa planted one white and two pink roses.

B Pippa planted one pink and two white roses.

C Pippa planted a pink rose straight after a white rose.

D Pippa planted a white rose straight after a pink rose.

2 A test was given to six people: Oliver, Hugo, Archie, Charlotte, Celine and Abigail. Hugo and Abigail got the same marks. Charlotte's mark was higher than Archie's but lower than Abigail's. Hugo's mark was higher than Celine's but lower than Oliver's.

Which is **not** true?

A Oliver got the highest mark.

B Hugo and Abigail were equal second.

C Celine must have come last.

D Archie got a lower mark than Hugo.

3 Matilda had to choose a different sport each term of the school year. The choices are:

Term 1	Term 2	Term 3	Term 4
cricket	softball	soccer	cricket
netball	basketball	netball	soccer
softball	tennis	hockey	tennis

Matilda chose netball, tennis, softball and cricket. Which **must** be correct?

A Matilda chose softball in term 1.

B Matilda chose tennis in term 2.

C Matilda chose netball in term 3.

D Matilda chose cricket in term 4.

4 Amelia, Daisy, Layla and Tia are 4 sisters. Amelia is older than Tia but younger than Daisy. Layla is younger than Daisy.

Which **must** be true?

A Tia is the youngest.

B Daisy is the oldest.

C Layla is the youngest.

D Amelia is the second oldest.

5 Hayden has a bag of 11 marbles. Three of the marbles are green, 4 are red and the rest are blue. Without looking, Hayden takes a marble from the bag.

Which of the statements below is/are correct?

1 Hayden is equally likely to take a red marble as a blue marble.

2 Hayden is more likely to take a blue marble than a green marble.

3 Hayden is less likely to take a green marble than a red marble.

A 1 only

B 3 only

C 1 and 3 only

D 1, 2 and 3

☞ **Answers and explanations on page 125**

Working with shapes

ACTIVITY: It is important to be familiar with both two- and three-dimensional shapes and objects. The features and properties must be known. Transformations, symmetry and nets should be understood. Students need to be able to visualise and manipulate the different shapes and objects.

SAMPLE QUESTION 1

Nadia is making a pattern by shading squares on a grid. When completed, the dashed line will be a line of symmetry.

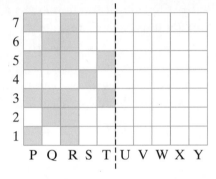

Which of these squares will **not** be shaded in the final design?

A U5   **B** V4   **C** W1   **D** X7   **E** Y3

STRATEGY

A line of symmetry is like a fold line where the two pieces match exactly. It is helpful to visualise what the finished design will look like.
Remember: We are looking for a square that will **not** be shaded. Don't rush and put down the first one that is shaded.

Work through each option, matching the squares on either side of the line of symmetry. So U5 will match T5 and, as T5 is shaded, U5 will also be in the finished pattern. V4 will match S4 so both will be shaded. W1 will match R1 and both will be shaded. X7 will match Q7. Q7 is not shaded so X7 will not be shaded either.
D is correct.

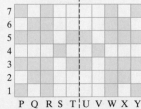

SAMPLE QUESTION 2

Amalia joins 7 cubes together to make this shape.

She picks up the shape and looks at it from all directions.

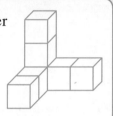

How many different faces can Amalia see?

A 28   **B** 29   **C** 30   **D** 35   **E** 42

STRATEGY

Seven cubes are joined together so some faces can be seen and some cannot. As each cube has 6 faces, the total number of faces, seen and unseen, is $7 \times 6 = 42$. One way to approach the problem is to work out how many faces can be seen from each direction. A second way is to work out how many faces cannot be seen and subtract that from 42. If there is time, you could do both methods and then be certain that the answer is correct.

Here if the object is viewed straight on from any of the six possible directions, five faces will be seen.

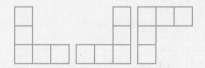

So the numbers of faces that can be seen is $6 \times 5 = 30$.

Alternatively, when any two cubes are joined the two faces that are joined together cannot be seen. There are 6 of those joins meaning that 12 faces cannot be seen: $42 - 12 = 30$. **C is correct.**

PRACTICE QUESTIONS

1 Which of these shapes have been joined together to make the shaded figure? They may have been used more than once.

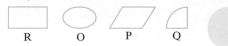

R   O   P   Q

A R + P   B O + R
C P + Q   D R + Q
E P + O

2 How many of the small shape will fit into the large one?

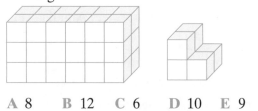

A 8   B 12   C 6   D 10   E 9

3 How many triangles can be found in this figure?

A 8   B 10   C 12   D 14   E 16

4 Nick made this object by sticking 10 cubes together.

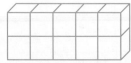

He then painted the whole of the object. Next he pulled the object apart into the 10 individual cubes. How many of those cubes have paint on exactly 3 faces?

A 0   B 2   C 4   D 6   E 8

5 This is a net of a normal dice. After Hannah rolls the dice, the 3 is on the top with 1 on the front face.

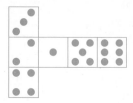

What is the sum of the numbers on the right side and back faces?

A 6   B 8   C 9   D 10   E 11

6 Which figure below shows the result when this shape is reflected in a vertical mirror?

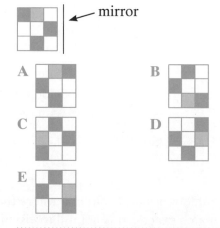

7 Here is the front view and right-side view of some books on a shelf:

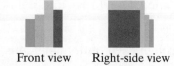

Front view   Right-side view

Which of these could be a view from the left side?

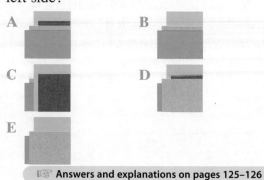

☞ **Answers and explanations on pages 125–126**

Working with numbers

ACTIVITY: It is very important to have a basic understanding of our number system. We need to be familiar with numbers and to be able to count, appreciate the concept of place value and be familiar with simple fractions. We also need to understand basic arithmetical processes and be confident working with numbers. We must solve simple problems and use reasoning to answer questions that require a little more thought than just straight adding or subtracting.

SAMPLE QUESTION 1

> The numbers 92, 28, 15, 76 and 34 are all rounded to the nearest ten.

For which number is the difference between the number and the rounded result the greatest?

A 92   **B** 28   **C** 15   **D** 76   **E** 34

STRATEGY

Reading the question carefully we can see that we are looking for the difference (remember that in maths the difference is found by subtracting the lower number from the higher one) between the numbers that are given and the result when they are rounded off. Here all the numbers have to be rounded to the nearest ten. Consider all the numbers one by one. Firstly 92 is between 90 and 100 and closest to 90. Next 28 is between 20 and 30, and closest to 30. 15 is halfway between 10 and 20. Remember: We have a rule that if a number ends in 5, it is rounded up so 15 would be rounded up to 20. 76 is between 70 and 80, and closest to 80. Finally 34 is between 30 and 40, and closest to 30.

Subtract to find the difference between each original number and its rounded result.

$92 - 90 = 2$; $30 - 28 = 2$; $20 - 15 = 5$; $80 - 76 = 4$; and $34 - 30 = 4$.

The biggest difference is 5. The number with the greatest difference between it and the rounded result is 15. **C is correct.**

Note that it is not necessary to round off all the numbers to find the greatest difference. It must be the number that is furthest from a multiple of 10.

SAMPLE QUESTION 2

> Tristan and Laura are playing a game. The person with the most points after 4 rounds is the winner. After the first round, Tristan has 23 more points than Laura but at the end of the game Laura wins with 105 points, 3 more than Tristan.

If Tristan scored 40 points in the first round, what might he have scored in the three other rounds?

A 28, 24, 20   **B** 22, 22, 17   **C** 18, 23, 22
D 26, 15, 21   **E** 27, 24, 13

STRATEGY

Read the question carefully and take time to think. Sometimes some of the information is not needed. So focus on the important points. The answer might be found by trial and error but if this method is used, there are often ways to simplify the working.

Here we know that Laura won with 105 points, 3 more than Tristan. Straight away we know that Tristan finished with 102 points. As $102 - 40$ is 62, Tristan must have 62 points from the other rounds. The question is simply asking which set of three numbers adds to 62. Rather than add the numbers in all the options, it can be made easier by just considering what 3 numbers add to a number ending in 2. So B (ends in 1), C (ends in 3) and E (ends in 4) cannot be the answer. As $3 \times 20 = 60$, A can easily be seen to add up to more than 62. The only possibility left is D and adding to check $26 + 15 + 21 = 62$. So Tristan might have scored 26, 15 and 21 in the other three rounds. **D is correct.**

PRACTICE QUESTIONS

1 What number is three thousands less than 41 827?

A 41 527 B 11 827
C 37 827 D 38 827
E 38 527

2 I pay $3030 for a motor boat and a trailer. If the motor boat costs twice as much as the trailer, how much was the trailer?

A $1015 B $1515
C $756 D $1010
E $2020

3 Johnny wins a small amount of money. He keeps $\frac{1}{4}$ himself and gives away the rest to his nephews and niece. His one niece and his nephews each receive $\frac{1}{8}$ of the money. How many nephews does Johnny have?

A 1 B 2 C 3 D 4 E 5

4 The sum of the numbers along each side of the triangle is the same.

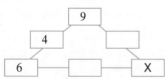

Using different numbers for each box and only numbers from 1–9, work out what number will go in the square marked X.

A 5 B 8 C 2 D 7 E 3

5 Judy, Ian and I were exploring an island when we came upon a treasure chest containing gold bars.

We left half in the chest, which we covered up with branches, and divided the rest up evenly among ourselves. I received 206 bars.

How many were there in the chest altogether?

A 824 B 1236 C 1030 D 618 E 1854

6 When Mario got on the school bus at his stop, 5 other children got on with him. At the next stop (the second last) 15 more got on and, at the last stop before school, 10 more got on. There were 75 children on the bus when it arrived at school.

How many children were on the bus when it arrived at Mario's stop?

A 34 B 36 C 44 D 46 E 54

7 What two signs should be in place of the ■ and ▲ in the number sentence?

3 ■ 3 ÷ 3 + 3 ▲ 3 = 3

A ×, − B +, ÷
C ×, ÷ D ÷, +
E +, −

8 The pattern in this diagram is 17 − 8 = 9.

The same pattern is used in this diagram but some numbers are missing and have been replaced with X, Y and Z.

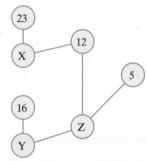

What is X + Y?

A 17 B 20
C 23 D 24
E 28

☞ **Answers and explanations on pages 126–127**

Working with measurements

ACTIVITY: It is very important to understand the basic units of measurement and be able to apply them in various situations. Questions might involve length, mass, capacity, perimeter or area. The ability to read and interpret the scales on measuring instruments is required.

SAMPLE QUESTION 1

Curtis needs 450 g of butter to make a cake. He has this amount on his scales.

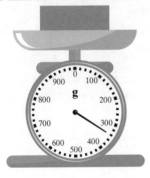

How much more butter does he need?

A 100 g B 110 g C 120 g D 130 g E 140 g

STRATEGY

The ability to be able to quickly, carefully and accurately read the scale on all types of measuring instruments is very important.

On these scales the amounts are in grams, as indicated by the g on the dial. The amounts every 100 g are shown on the dial. There are 4 marks between each amount, making 5 gaps or divisions altogether. So each of the shorter marks shows 100 g ÷ 5 or 20 g. We can count by 20s as we move around the dial.

Here the arrow is pointing to 340 so there is currently 340 g of butter on the scale. As Curtis needs 450 g, he needs an extra 110 g (450 − 340 = 110). **B is correct.**

SAMPLE QUESTION 2

Dylan is planting a straight line of trees next to the fence along one side of his property. First he plants a tree at each end of the property and then he plants a tree halfway between those two trees. Next Dylan plants trees halfway between those he has already planted. Finally he again plants a tree halfway between all the trees he has already planted. When he has finished the trees are 10 metres apart.

How long is that side of Dylan's property?

A 60 m B 70 m C 80 m D 90 m E 100 m

STRATEGY

With questions that are quite involved, often a diagram can help students visualise what is required. Here, to begin with, there are trees planted at each end of the property.

●   ●

Next a tree is planted between those:

●   ●   ●

Then trees are planted halfway between those:

●   ●   ●   ●   ●

And, finally, halfway between those:

●   ●   ●   ●   ●   ●   ●   ●   ●

So there are 9 trees and 8 gaps between them.

Each gap is 10 m. As 8 × 10 = 80, the side of the property must be 80 m long. **C is correct.**

1 The distance from Newcastle to Sydney is 150 km. Train P leaves Newcastle travelling at 75 km an hour and train Q leaves Sydney at the same time travelling at 60 km an hour. Which correctly completes this statement?

Train P will reach Sydney

A at the same time as train Q reaches Newcastle.

B $\frac{1}{2}$ hour before train Q reaches Newcastle.

C 1 hour before train Q reaches Newcastle.

D $\frac{1}{2}$ hour after train Q reaches Newcastle.

E 1 hour after train Q reaches Newcastle.

2 At her school athletics carnival, in the long jump Sophie jumped 3 m 45 cm for her first jump, 3 m 27 cm for her second jump and 3 m 33 cm for her third. How far short of 12 m did she jump altogether?

A 2 m

B 1 m 85 cm

C 2 m 5 cm

D 1 m 55 cm

E 1 m 95 cm

3 A tiler is retiling a bathroom floor because some tiles have been damaged. The blue tiles are good enough to keep as they are, but the grey space needs new tiles. How many **more** tiles must the tiler buy?

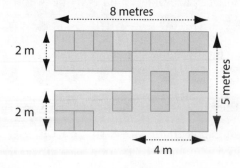

A 11

B 20

C 15

D 21

E 25

4 Both of these jugs have water in them as shown.

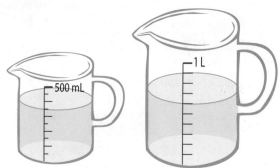

How much **more** water is in the larger jug than the smaller jug?

A 50 mL

B 250 mL

C 300 mL

D 350 mL

E 500 mL

5 In the high jump at her school sports day, Kylie jumps 15 cm higher than anyone else. The bar starts at 90 cm and goes up by 10 cm twice, then 5 cm three times till everybody else is eliminated (fails the height). How high did Kylie clear?

A 1 m 30 cm

B 1 m 35 cm

C 1 m 40 cm

D 1 m 45 cm

E 1 m 50 cm

6 Buttons are to be placed every 8 cm along the edge of a strip of material. The first button will be at the top of the material and the final button at the bottom. The material is 1.6 m long.

How many buttons will be needed?

A 15   B 18

C 20   D 21

E 24

☞ **Answers and explanations on pages 127–128**

Working with time and dates

ACTIVITY: Time can be a difficult concept. It is important to have an understanding of time expressed in different forms. Students need to be able to find the passage of time between different events, including working with dates and calculating time differences.

SAMPLE QUESTION 1

Douglas and Coral both competed in a car rally. Douglas began one section at 10 am and completed it at 10:50 am. Coral completed the same section at 2:30 pm. Her time was twice as fast as Douglas's.

What time did Coral begin that section?

A 12:50 pm   B 1:05 pm
C 1:50 pm   D 1:55 pm
E 2:05 pm

STRATEGY

Reading carefully we can see there are a few parts to the question. We need to find the amount of time Douglas and Coral took, then work backwards from Coral's given finishing time to find her starting time.

Douglas began at 10 am and finished at 10:50 am so he took 50 minutes to complete the section.

Coral was twice as fast as Douglas so she completed the section in half the time.

$50 \div 2 = 25$ so Coral took 25 minutes.

Coral finished at 2:30 pm, meaning she started 25 minutes before 2:30 pm.

So Coral started at 2:05 pm. **E is correct.**

SAMPLE QUESTION 2

This month Ashleigh is appearing in a play. The play is on every night from Thursday 5 to Sunday 22 except for Monday and Tuesday nights. Every Wednesday and Saturday there is also an afternoon performance as well as the night one.

How many performances are there altogether?

A 17   B 18   C 19   D 20   E 21

STRATEGY

It is important to read the question carefully and make sure you understand what is happening. Don't overlook any important information.

Here we know there are performances on 5 nights every week plus 2 afternoons so there are 7 performances every week.

Counting forward by 7s we know that Thursday 12 will start the second week and Thursday 19 will start the third week. From Thursday 5 until Wednesday 18 is two full weeks so that will mean 14 performances. There are then performances on Thursday 19, Friday 20, two on Saturday 21 and one on Sunday 22. That is another 5 performances.

So the total number of performances is $14 + 5 = 19$. **C is correct.**

PRACTICE QUESTIONS

1 A bus is due to leave its depot at 11:00 am. It stops first at Elizabeth Street at 11:10 am, then at Liverpool Street at 11:35 am. From there it takes 35 minutes to reach Sussex Street, then another 25 minutes to Druitt Street. The next bus leaves half an hour later. At what time will the second bus arrive at the Druitt Street stop?

A 12:05 am

B 1:55 pm

C 12:55 pm

D 1:05 pm

E 12:05 pm

2 The year 2020 was a leap year. If 15 February was a Saturday, what day of the week was 7 March?

A Thursday

B Friday

C Saturday

D Sunday

E Monday

3 Cathy left home to go to work at half past seven in the morning. When she returned home her clock read 17:15. How long was Cathy away from home?

A 9 h 45 min

B 10 h 15 min

C 10 h 45 min

D 11 h 45 min

E 12 h 15 min

4 Cooper left work at 5:45 pm one day and went back to work at 9:15 am the next day. How long was Cooper away from work?

A $3\frac{1}{2}$ h   B $4\frac{1}{2}$ h

C $14\frac{1}{2}$ h   D $15\frac{1}{2}$ h

E $16\frac{1}{2}$ h

5 Mila left home at 9:45 am. She walked to a friend's house, arriving at 10:30 am. Later Mila caught a bus home. The return journey was three times faster than the outward journey.

If Mila arrived home at 2:15 pm, how long did she spend at her friend's house?

A 2 h 30 min

B 2 h 45 min

C 3 h 15 min

D 3 h 30 min

E 4 h 30 min

6 The choir will be performing carols on Monday, Thursday and Saturday each week beginning on Monday 4 December and finishing on 21 December. There will be extra performances on 19 and 20 December.

How many performances will there be altogether?

A 9   B 10   C 11   D 12   E 13

7 Toby's grandparents were married on Saturday 26 March, 1988. They moved into their home on 10 May 1988. On what day of the week did they move into their home?

A Monday   B Tuesday

C Wednesday   D Thursday

E Friday

☞ Answers and explanations on page 128

Working with graphs

ACTIVITY: This involves interpreting the representation of material in a graphic or symbolic form; that is, in a graph. It tests perceptual and numerical skills and is a form of abstract thinking.

SAMPLE QUESTION 1

The number of children absent from school is shown in a graph each week. The graphs for two weeks are given here but the number absent on Tuesday is missing from the second graph.

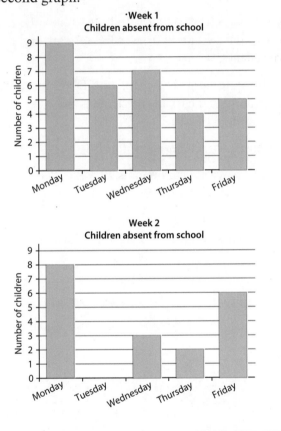

·Week 1
Children absent from school

Week 2
Children absent from school

If there were 5 more children absent in week 1 than in week 2, how many children were absent on Tuesday in week 2?

A 1   B 5   C 6   D 7   E 12

STRATEGY

You need to understand two graphs and interpret the required information.

Here each graph tells us how many children were absent on each day of the week. We can find how many students were absent each day and hence the total number absent for each week.

In week 1 the number of children absent was 9 on Monday, 6 on Tuesday, 7 on Wednesday, 4 on Thursday and 5 on Friday.

$9 + 6 + 7 + 4 + 5 = 31$

So, in total, 31 children were absent in week 1. This was 5 more than the number absent in week 2 so there must have been 26 absent in week 2. In week 2 the number absent was 8 on Monday, 3 on Wednesday, 2 on Thursday and 6 on Friday.
$8 + 3 + 2 + 6 = 19$ and $26 - 19 = 7$. So 7 students must have been absent on Tuesday in week 2.
D is correct.

An alternative method would be to compare how many children were absent on individual days. For example, there was 1 more student absent on Monday in week 1 than in week 2. There were 4 more on Wednesday, 2 more on Thursday and 1 less on Friday. There must also have been 1 less on Tuesday to make 5 more in total.

Working with graphs

SAMPLE QUESTION 2

The people living in all the houses in a street were asked how many cars were owned by people living at each house. The graph shows the results:

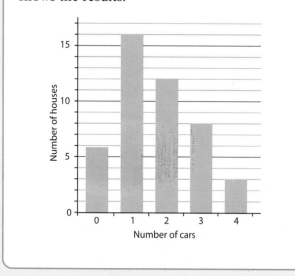

Which statement is **not** correct?

A There were 12 houses that had exactly 2 cars.

B Twice as many houses had no cars than had 4 cars.

C Half as many houses had 3 cars than had 1 car.

D Together the number of houses that had 1 car plus the number of houses that had 3 cars is the same as twice the number of houses that had 2 cars.

E There was a total of 45 cars belonging to people in the street.

STRATEGY

This question requires interpretation of the graph and consideration of each of the statements in the options to determine whether they are true or false.

The number of cars per house is given along the horizontal axis and these range from 0 to 4.

The vertical axis gives the number of houses that have each of those number of cars.

So 6 houses have no cars, 16 houses have 1 car, 12 houses have 2 cars, 8 houses have 3 cars and 3 houses have 4 cars.

So the statements in A, B, C and D are all correct. The number of cars in the street is not immediately obvious.

16 houses with 1 car is a total of 16 cars.

12 houses with 2 cars means $12 \times 2 = 24$ cars and 8 houses with 3 cars is $8 \times 3 = 24$ cars.

So it quickly becomes obvious there are more than 45 cars altogether. E is not a correct statement.

3 houses with 4 cars means $3 \times 4 = 12$ cars. The total number is $16 + 24 + 24 + 12$, or 76.
E is the correct answer.

1   The number of children who did extra
subjects after school was recorded in a
table. A graph was then drawn of the
results but it was not labelled.

Art	62	Chess	35
Carpentry	86	Swimming	55
Drama	44	Tennis	30

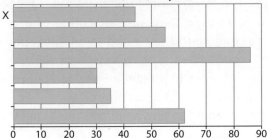

After-school (extra) subjects

On the graph, which category of after-
school subjects is the bar marked X?

A Art   B Swimming
C Chess   D Drama
E Tennis

2   A company makes six different products
and this graph shows the proportion of
sales for each of those.

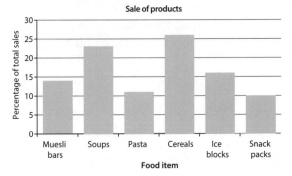

Sale of products

A manager at the company made the
following statements. Which is/are correct?

X   Nearly one-quarter of all sales are
soups.

Y   Sales of muesli bars and snack
packs together are greater than
sales of cereals.

Z   Sales of soups and ice blocks
together make up more than half of
all sales.

A X only

B Y only

C Z only

D Both X and Y

E Both X and Z

3   In Nicknack Primary School the
sportsmistress counted the number of
children in the different age groups and
came up with the following figures:

8 years	9 years	10 years	11 years	12 years
34	70	86	101	and over 65

The sportsmaster preferred to give the
numbers to the principal in the form of a
graph and he produced the one below.

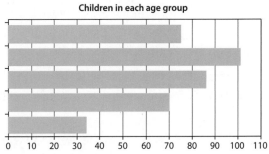

Children in each age group

He got one of the numbers wrong on his
graph. Which one?

A 12 years and over

B 9 years

C 8 years

D 10 years

E 11 years

☞ **Answers and explanations on page 128**

Read the text below then answer the questions

The Velveteen Rabbit

For a long time he lived in the toy cupboard or on the nursery floor, and no one thought very much about him. He was naturally shy, and being only made of velveteen, some of the more expensive toys quite snubbed him. The mechanical toys were very superior, and looked down upon everyone else; they were full of modern ideas, and pretended they were real. The model boat, who had lived through two seasons and lost most of his paint, caught the tone from them and never missed an opportunity of referring to his rigging in technical terms. The Rabbit could not claim to be a model of anything, for he didn't know that real rabbits existed; he thought they were all stuffed with sawdust like himself, and he understood that sawdust was quite out-of-date and should never be mentioned in modern circles. Even Timothy, the jointed wooden lion, who was made by the disabled soldiers, and should have had broader views, put on airs and pretended he was connected with Government. Between them all the poor little Rabbit was made to feel himself very insignificant and commonplace, and the only person who was kind to him at all was the Skin Horse.

The Skin Horse had lived longer in the nursery than any of the others. He was so old that his brown coat was bald in patches and showed the seams underneath, and most of the hairs in his tail had been pulled out to string bead necklaces. He was wise, for he had seen a long succession of mechanical toys arrive to boast and swagger, and by-and-by break their mainsprings and pass away, and he knew that they were only toys, and would never turn into anything else. For nursery magic is very strange and wonderful, and only those playthings that are old and wise and experienced like the Skin Horse understand all about it.

'What is REAL?' asked the Rabbit one day, when they were lying side by side near the nursery fender, before Nana came to tidy the room. 'Does it mean having things that buzz inside you and a stick-out handle?'

'Real isn't how you are made,' said the Skin Horse. 'It's a thing that happens to you. When a child loves you for a long, long time, not just to play with, but REALLY loves you, then you become Real.'

'Does it hurt?' asked the Rabbit.

'Sometimes,' said the Skin Horse, for he was always truthful. 'When you are Real you don't mind being hurt.'

'Does it happen all at once, like being wound up,' he asked, 'or bit by bit?'

'It doesn't happen all at once,' said the Skin Horse. 'You become. It takes a long time. That's why it doesn't happen often to people who break easily, or have sharp edges, or who have to be carefully kept. Generally, by the time you are Real, most of your hair has been loved off, and your eyes drop out and you get loose in the joints and very shabby. But these things don't matter at all, because once you are Real you can't be ugly, except to people who don't understand.'

'I suppose *you* are real?' said the Rabbit. And then he wished he had not said it, for he thought the Skin Horse might be sensitive. But the Skin Horse only smiled.

SAMPLE TEST

'The Boy's Uncle made me Real,' he said. 'That was a great many years ago; but once you are Real you can't become unreal again. It lasts for always.'

The Rabbit sighed. He thought it would be a long time before this magic called Real happened to him. He longed to become Real, to know what it felt like; and yet the idea of growing shabby and losing his eyes and whiskers was rather sad. He wished that he could become it without these uncomfortable things happening to him.

From *The Velveteen Rabbit* by Marjorie Wilson

For questions **1–5**, choose the option (**A**, **B**, **C** or **D**) which you think best answers the question.

1   The mechanical toys thought of the other toys as

   A inferior.
   B better made.
   C worthy of admiration.
   D wiser.

2   What do the mechanical toys, the model boat and Timothy have in common?

   A They like the Skin Horse.
   B They are getting old and worn.
   C They all put on airs.
   D They pretend to be real.

3   What does the Skin Horse understand that most toys don't?

   A why you grow old
   B how you become real
   C why things buzz inside you
   D how to get repaired

4   The conversation between the Rabbit and the Skin Horse is

   A playful and enjoyable.
   B solemn and business-like.
   C friendly and lighthearted.
   D intense and meaningful.

5   The Rabbit is a likeable character mainly because he is

   A insignificant and commonplace.
   B humble and considerate.
   C made of velveteen.
   D friendly and outgoing.

☞ **Answers and explanations on pages 129–131**

SAMPLE TEST

Read the poem below by James Armitage then answer the questions.

Tidal

Cheek to the wind

And hair wild streaming.

Free on the sand

With the gulls screaming.

Out in the estuary strayed

Lost in the dreaming

I suddenly find

The forgotten tide

From its sleep emerging

Snide and snarling

Turned on me surging

Eager tongue curling

Pursuing me—nowhere to hide;

Then just beyond

Its grasp fast swirling

I stagger ashore

Chastened and pondering

Still struggling to understand

How I did ignore

Such portents of danger

When wandering so far from the land.

© James Armitage; reproduced with permission

For questions **6–9**, choose the option (**A**, **B**, **C** or **D**) which you think best answers the question.

6 The wind in the opening two lines is

A teasing.

B deafening.

C forceful.

D playful.

7 Why does the poet forget about the dangers of the tide?

A He isn't thinking about where he is.

B He thinks the tide has gone out.

C The seagulls are drowning out its noise.

D The wind is distracting him from how the water is behaving.

8 The poet makes the tide sound like

A a scary seagull flapping at him.

B a memory from a lost dream.

C a distant storm.

D an angry monster chasing after him.

9 What are 'portents of danger'?

A dreams of the future

B doors you shouldn't open

C important moments

D warning signs that danger is ahead

☞ **Answers and explanations on pages 129–131**

SAMPLE TEST

Read the text below then answer the questions.

Five sentences have been removed from the text. Choose from the sentences (**A–F**) the one which fits each gap (**10–14**). There is one extra sentence which you do not need to use.

Advertising and children

It took a long time for children to be targeted directly by advertisers. **10** _____ At that time, several toys that were to become classics were on the market—the frisbee, the Barbie doll and the hula hoop—helped on their way by this form of advertising.

In 1952 a television commercial was made for a toy called Mr Potato Head. It showed real children playing excitedly with, and talking about, their new toy. **11** _____ Around 1955 other toy commercials were shown on the *Mickey Mouse Club* and the trend of appealing directly to children took hold. Today, targeting children directly is a multibillion-dollar industry.

Children are good targets for advertisers because they influence family spending and spend money themselves. Furthermore they are very brand conscious. **12** _____ As they grow up they quickly learn which brands are in favour with their peers.

However, there has been debate about the dangers involved in targeting young children in this way. **13** _____ It is also thought they set up unrealistic goals and stereotypes and turn children into consumer addicts.

One study published in 2010 in the *American Journal of Public Health* surveyed children's television viewing in Australia, Asia, Western Europe, and North and South America. The researchers concluded children were regularly exposed to a high volume of advertising of unhealthy foods.

They also noted that persuasive techniques likely to be effective with children were used. **14** _____ As a result the researchers recommended that the nature of advertising screened in children's peak viewing times be regulated.

A	This was of concern due to research indicating children under 8 years tend to accept advertising as truthful.
B	One of the earliest attempts at persuading children to want a product was an American television ad released in the 1950s.
C	Advertising, as an industry, did not really gain traction until the arrival of mass media.
D	Claims have been made that such advertisements often promote unhealthy choices and are a factor in causing childhood obesity.
E	The original version of the toy consisted of facial features and body parts that could be stuck into a potato.
F	Young children, for example, recognise advertising signs and slogans from a very early age.

☞ Answers and explanations on pages 129–131

SAMPLE TEST

Read the four texts below on the theme of insects.

For questions **15–20**, choose the option (**A**, **B**, **C** or **D**) which you think best answers the question.

Which text ...

describes an insect that excels at keeping hidden? 15 _____

does not include a reference to scientific research? 16 _____

discusses an insect that has grown smaller in size over time? 17 _____

refers to an insect that sometimes causes harm to its environment? 18 _____

describes an insect that depends on its flying ability for survival? 19 _____

is about insects who represent humans? 20 _____

TEXT A

Dragonflies evolved around 300 million years ago. Modern dragonflies have wingspans of about five to twelve cm but the wingspans of some fossilised dragonflies reached almost 60 cm.

The body of the adult dragonfly is often brightly coloured while its wings are transparent and embedded with tiny black veins. Each wing can be moved independently of the other. Large, bulbous eyes, with several thousand facets, give the dragonfly excellent sight. They can detect a wider range of colours than humans.

A dragonfly can fly swiftly or hover, and fly in any direction including sideways or backwards. It catches its food while on the wing. Scientists study its flying abilities with an eye to reproducing them in products such as flying robots.

TEXT B

I have just read a book about ants. Well not exactly about ants in the sense that it gives you information about them. It is a story about an army of ants who go on an expedition. It is called *The March of the Ants* by Ursula Dubosarsky, illustrated by Tohby Riddle.

The Chief Ant asks the ants what they are going to bring on their expedition. Food, says the first; water, says the second; and so on. Then the littlest ant says she will bring her book. The Chief Ant tries to dissuade her. What use could a book possibly be, he asks.

I'm not going to tell you what happens on their very long, trying expedition or whether or not the littlest ant regrets her decision. But I do hope you'll read the story to find out.

☞ **Answers and explanations on pages 129–131**

TEXT C

Stick insects, or phasmids (from the Greek word for ghost or phantom), are found in most countries in the world. There are about 150 species of stick insect in Australia. They vary in length ranging from a few centimetres to around 27 cm and look like sticks or leaves. Their appearance makes for an excellent camouflage which keeps them safe from predators. Some species also suddenly reveal brightly coloured wings or spray toxic chemicals at their enemies.

Like all insects, stick insects have six legs but their legs are unusual in that each can move independently of the other. In fact, researchers have studied the way stick insects walk so they can apply what they learn to the development of walking robots.

Stick insects are herbivorous. What they eat is helpful in balancing ecosystems. Many species live in eucalypt trees. Very occasionally they occur in plague numbers. When this happens, they can cause great damage to eucalypt forests.

TEXT D

Human beings thought they invented gears. New research shows that nature got there first. A planthopper is an insect of about half a centimetre in size. It feeds by sucking the contents out of plants. On the top of each leg, where the hind legs join its body, you can see a row of small interlocking teeth. When a planthopper jumps, these teeth make its legs rotate and extend at the same time. They work like gears!

Scientists in the UK studied the insects' movements using a high-speed camera with a microscope attached. They put the insects on their backs and tickled their tummies to make them kick. They found their hind legs could move within a millionth of a second of each other. Their legs being connected by the gears helps them to jump faster and further. Now high precision machines, such as 3D printing machines, are making it possible to create tiny gears similar to those found on young planthoppers.

1 A cube has squares, circles and triangles on its faces. Opposite faces have the same symbol. Which one of these could be the net of that cube?

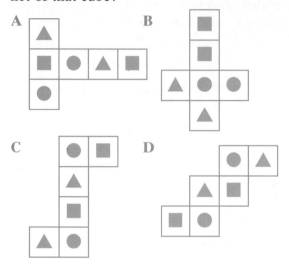

2 Lucy's teacher told the class: 'To have even a chance of receiving a School Citizenship Award you must have participated in at least five school community activities during the year.'

If Lucy's teacher is correct, which one of these statements will be true?

A All of the students who have participated in five school community activities during the year will receive a School Citizenship Award.

B Only the students who have participated in five school community activities during the year will receive a School Citizenship Award.

C None of the students who have participated in less than five school community activities during the year will receive a School Citizenship Award.

D Some of the students who have participated in less than five school community activities during the year might receive a School Citizenship Award.

3 Bill is 2 cm taller than Heidi. Frank is 4 cm shorter than Heidi and I am exactly between Bill and Frank. How tall am I?

A 4 cm shorter than Frank

B 1 cm taller than Heidi

C 1 cm shorter than Heidi

D 4 cm shorter than Bill

4

Nina: 'Jack had better run! There's a tiger right behind him!'

Which assumption is needed for Nina's conclusion to work?

A Jack likes tigers.

B The tiger is very close to Jack.

C The tiger is a toy.

D The tiger is not in a cage.

5 This month a television show will be screened from Sunday to Friday each week, beginning on Sunday 9. The last show will be on Sunday 30 and the show will go for an hour on weekdays and an hour and a half on Sundays. For how many hours will the show be screened altogether?

A $19\frac{1}{2}$ hours   B 21 hours

C $24\frac{1}{2}$ hours   D 26 hours

Answers and explanations on pages 131–132

6 Each of these squares has five different shapes arranged to fill the square.

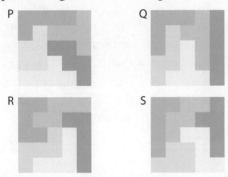

Which two squares have the most shapes in common? The shapes may be turned around or over.

A P and Q   B Q and R
C R and S   D P and S

7 A cricket coach says: 'All players should wear a mouthguard during training and games.'

Which one of these statements, if true, best supports the coach's claim?

A Players in other teams have always worn mouthguards.

B Mouthguards protect teeth and help prevent jaw injuries.

C The coach's team is playing well this season.

D Mouthguards are cheap and easily available.

8 Conor's uncle is in the bookstore.

Conor's uncle: 'I want to get my nephew a book for his birthday. He said he saw the one he wants on display but I can't seem to find it. He said it's about dinosaurs and has a green cover.'

Sales assistant: 'This one has a green cover and is about dinosaurs—it must be the one your nephew wants!'

Which one of the following sentences shows the mistake the sales assistant has made?

A Conor might now prefer a book about trucks.

B Even if the book has a green cover, it might not be about dinosaurs.

C There might be more than one book with a green cover about dinosaurs.

D Conor might have seen the book in the library, not the bookstore.

9 Oliver and Ava arrived at Fenton station at the same time, 4 pm. Oliver came by train from Greenhill which he left at 1:30 pm. Ava came by bus from Windrush. Oliver's trip was 5 times longer than Ava's. At what time did Ava leave Windrush?

A 3:30 pm   B 3 pm
C 2:30 pm   D 2 pm

☞ Answers and explanations on pages 131–132

SAMPLE TEST

10 Whenever Uma's dog Patch gets a new toy, she always gets excited. And when Patch is excited, she always runs around in circles chasing her tail.

Anh: 'If you give Patch that toy, she's sure to run around in circles chasing her tail.'

Ruby: 'I saw Patch running around in circles chasing her tail yesterday—she must have a new toy!'

If the information in the box is true, whose reasoning is correct?

A Anh only

B Ruby only

C Both Anh and Ruby

D Neither Anh nor Ruby

11 A piece of paper is folded in half (the top being brought down to the bottom) and a crease mark is made along the fold line. Without unfolding the paper, the process is repeated and repeated again. Then the paper is unfolded and the crease lines are found to be 3 cm apart. **How long** is the piece of paper?

A 21 cm   B 24 cm   C 27 cm   D 30 cm

12 A recipe for shortbread uses 450 g of flour, 300 g of icing sugar, 2 tablespoons of ground rice and 350 g of butter to make 60 biscuits. Nelly has 1 kg of flour, 500 g of icing sugar, 3 tablespoons of ground rice and 750 g of butter.

What is the greatest number of biscuits Nelly can make using this recipe with the ingredients that she has?

A 60   B 75   C 90   D 120

13

An environmentalist says: 'We need to save our world's butterflies and moths.'

Which one of these statements, if true, best supports the environmentalist's claim?

A There are over 230 000 species of butterflies and moths around the world.

B In the last decade there has been a 50% decline in butterfly and moth populations.

C An interactive map and database of moth and butterfly photos is being created.

D Butterflies and moths are fragile and beautiful.

☞ **Answers and explanations on pages 131–132**

SAMPLE TEST

14 Melia's family is discussing what they want to do in the holidays. Melia's mum wants to garden, go fishing, watch a movie, go bushwalking and sleep in. Melia's dad wants to make bread, sleep in and go bushwalking. Melia wants to go fishing, read, go bushwalking, go surfing and sleep in.

What activities does Melia's mum want to do that neither Melia nor her dad want to do?

A surf and make bread

B watch a movie and go bushwalking

C garden and watch a movie

D go fishing and garden

15 Some students did three tests, each marked out of 50. Here are their results. Isabella's mark in the third test is missing.

Name	Test 1	Test 2	Test 3
Isabella	44	42	
Jordan	42	41	46
Harper	47	38	42
Mary	45	40	43
Paige	39	43	48

A prize is awarded to the person with the highest total for the three tests. What is the lowest mark that Isabella can score to win the prize?

A 43   **B** 45   **C** 47   **D** 49

16 Six friends—Pia, Quentin, Rhianna, Samuel, Tara and Umar—are standing in a field. Rhianna is east of Quentin and north of Samuel. Tara is west of Samuel and south of Pia. Pia is north-west of Rhianna and north-east of Umar. Who is south-east of Quentin?

A Samuel **B** Umar **C** Pia   **D** Tara

17 A politician says: 'Black rhinos are critically endangered so we must try to save them.'

Which assumption has the politician made in order to draw their conclusion?

A Saving black rhinos would be a good thing.

B Black rhinos are critically endangered.

C Black rhinos must be saved.

D We cannot save all endangered species.

18 Ms Brown told the class: 'To have any chance of going on the excursion to the art gallery next week you must watch the movie about Australian artists at lunchtime today in the library.'

Oliver: 'I have chess club at lunchtime today but I'll tell Ms Brown so I'll still be able to go on the art gallery excursion.'

Suma: 'I'm going to watch the movie in the library at lunchtime today so I'll definitely be able to go on the art gallery excursion.'

If the information in the box is true, whose reasoning is correct?

A Oliver only

B Suma only

C Both Oliver and Suma

D Neither Oliver nor Suma

☞ Answers and explanations on pages 131–132

19 A contestant on a TV game show is made to wear a blindfold and then gets to choose one briefcase out of five to win whatever prize it contains. Four of the cases have 'booby prizes' (pieces of fruit) but one contains $1000. The contestant has won some clues as she played the game and should be able to win the money.

These are the clues:

- There is one case between the red case and the money.
- The blue case is to the right of the red case.
- The gold case is at the far left and there is one case between it and the red case.
- The silver case is not next to the red case.
- The green case is not next to the case with the money.

Which case should the contestant choose?

A blue   B gold   C green   D silver

20 Uri's class wanted to choose an animal for the class to symbolically adopt. They decided to hold a vote. Class members could vote for a platypus, a koala or a Tasmanian devil. Everyone got two votes but they could not vote for the same animal twice. The teacher said they would only adopt an animal if everyone in the class voted for it. If this did not happen, they would choose a different type of charity option instead. Every animal got at least one vote.

Knowing **one** of the following would allow us to know the result of the vote. Which one is it?

A Every student voted for either koala or Tasmanian devil or both.

B The platypus was the most popular vote.

C No student voted for both koala and platypus.

D Only two students voted for koala.

☞ **Answers and explanations on pages 131–132**

1 Millie is going to shade three-quarters of this shape. She has already shaded three squares.

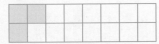

How many more squares need to be shaded?

A 8   B 9   C 10   D 11   E 12

2 Logan has made a graph of the number of wet days each month from January to November.

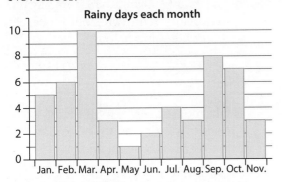

What is the smallest number of days it must rain in December so that there are more wet days in the second half of the year than the first?

A 1   B 2   C 3   D 4   E 5

3 Today is Friday 7 January. Ella's birthday is on 15 February. On what day of the week is Ella's birthday this year?

A Monday   B Tuesday
C Wednesday   D Thursday
E Friday

4 Part of a design is shown. When completed the design will have both horizontal and vertical lines of symmetry. What will be the area, in squares, of the finished pattern?

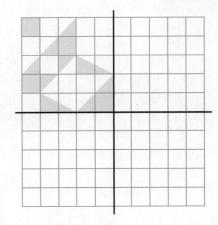

A 36   B 38   C 40   D 50   E 60

5 What is the amount I have saved if I have exactly two of each kind of Australian coin in my money box?

A $7.70   B $8.70
C $7.60   D $7.30
E $6.70

6 Selina has a set of cards showing the numbers from 1 to 9.

| 1 | 2 | 3 | 4 | 5 | 6 | 7 | 8 | 9 |

Without looking, Selina takes a card from the set. Which of these statements is/are true?

X   Selina is more likely to take an odd number than an even one.

Y   Selina is equally likely to take a number greater than five as a number less than five.

Z   Selina is less likely to take a card showing 4 than a card showing 9.

A X only

B Y only

C Z only

D X and Y only

E Y and Z only

☞ **Answers and explanations on pages 133–134**

7 Harry added the numbers 37 and 56 and then rounded the answer to the nearest ten. William rounded 37 to the nearest ten and then rounded 56 to the nearest ten and then added his two answers. What is the difference between Harry and William's final answers?

A 0   **B** 5   **C** 7   **D** 10   **E** 20

8 Which number is missing in this sequence?

110   100   91   **?**   76   70

A 84   **B** 81   **C** 85   **D** 83   **E** 82

9 ♦ represents a number.

82 − ♦ = 37 + 26

What **number** does ♦ represent?

A 19   **B** 23   **C** 29   **D** 63   **E** 71

10 Frances caught a plane that left Sydney 10 minutes before midday on Tuesday. When she finally reached her destination, Frances calculated that the time in Sydney would be 25 minutes before 7 am on Wednesday. How long did it take Frances to reach her destination?

A $6\frac{1}{4}$ hours   **B** $6\frac{3}{4}$ hours

C $16\frac{1}{4}$ hours   **D** $18\frac{1}{4}$ hours

E $18\frac{3}{4}$ hours

11 A piece of wire is bent to form a square. Each side of the square is 10 cm long. The wire is then straightened out and bent to form a rectangle. Two sides of the rectangle are each 12 cm long. How long is each of the other two sides?

A 4 cm   **B** 6 cm

C 8 cm   **D** 10 cm

E 12 cm

12 Susan wants to buy some rice. It is sold in packets of 500 g for $2 or 2 kg for $7.

What is the lowest price Susan can pay for 5 kg of the rice?

A $16   **B** $17   **C** $18   **D** $19   **E** $20

13 Mr Judd is a salesman living in Freetown. Each weekday he travels to a different one of the nearby towns, then home again. The distances to each town from Freetown are given in the table below:

Sprint 78 km	Gallap 37 km	Kantor 49km
Trott 95 km	Riggal 57 km	

If Mr Judd travels a total of 286 km on Monday, Tuesday and Wednesday, which three towns has he visited?

A Sprint, Kantor, Riggal

B Gallap, Trott, Riggal

C Gallap, Kantor, Riggal

D Kantor, Trott, Sprint

E Sprint, Gallap, Trott

14 In a sequence, each number is one more than double the previous number. Nate added the number before 63 in the sequence to the number after 63. What was his answer?

A 146   **B** 147   **C** 157   **D** 158   **E** 159

☞ **Answers and explanations on pages 133–134**

SAMPLE TEST

15 From the alphabet Molly picked out these letters that use only horizontal and vertical lines.

If Molly chooses three different letters from these, what is the greatest number of right angles her letters might have?

A 12 B 11 C 9 D 8 E 7

16 The numbers 5, 6, 7, 8 and 9 are to be written in the five circles, one number in each circle. The 3 numbers in the two lines add to 22.

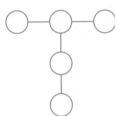

What number will go in the circle that lies in both lines?

A 5 B 6 C 7 D 8 E 9

17 Greta has a piece of paper in the shape of a triangle.

Which of these shapes can Greta not make by folding the triangle in just one place?

A   B

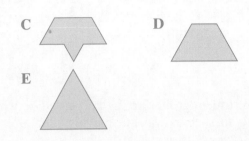

C   D

E

18 Some of the numbers are missing in this magic square.

16		8
		4

When completed, the numbers in every row, every column and both diagonals will add to 30.

Which number will go in the shaded square?

A 2 B 6 C 10 D 14 E 18

19 Charlotte emptied her piggy bank. It contained only 5-, 10-, 20- and 50-cent coins and there were at least two of each of those. Altogether, she had $9.30 and there were eleven 50-cent coins.

What is the greatest number of 20-cent coins Charlotte can have?

A 16 B 17 C 18 D 19 E 20

20 Daisy has two bottles. When full, one holds 3 litres and the other 5 litres, but there are no other markings to accurately measure amounts. Daisy has no other containers but plenty of water to fill and refill the bottles and can throw the water out at any time. Which of the following amounts can Daisy accurately measure using her bottles?

A 2 L only   B 1 or 2 L only
C 1 or 4 L only D 2 or 4 L only
E 1, 2 or 4 L

☞ Answers and explanations on pages 133–134

PRACTICE QUESTIONS

1 D   2 C Page 5

1   The student groups are named based on what they do, such as drawing, playing with plasticine or playing cards when the teacher's assistant is not there. The 'plasticine' desk group refers to the group of students who play with plasticine in her absence.

A and B are incorrect. Nothing in the classroom is made of plasticine.

C is incorrect. Playing with plasticine is an escape from schoolwork for that group.

2   Shuxuan knows Sen hasn't seen the teacher's assistant because she is so involved in her card game. She warns Sen of her arrival by pressing her elbow into her arm.

A is incorrect. To make Sen laugh would draw attention to her and this is the opposite of what Shuxuan wants to achieve.

B is incorrect. There is no evidence that Shuxuan is clumsy.

D is incorrect. This is the opposite of what Shuxuan wants. Shuxuan knows if the teacher's assistant sees Sen's cards on the table, she will get into trouble.

1 C   2 A   Page 8

1   **A is incorrect.** The narrator shifts indecisively between possibilities of what she might do with her hair and ends up putting off the decision.

B is incorrect. Although the narrator is obsessed with her hair, this is because she feels dissatisfied with how she looks not because she is vain.

D is incorrect. The narrator shows herself to be fearful rather than fearless about changing her hairstyle.

2   Dad's suggestion of a Mohawk is likely to be a joke and a way of teasing his daughter as she dithers between possibilities. Her Mum's

strong rejection of his choice of hairstyle (something that 'sticks up high and straight') confirms this.

The other options are incorrect.

1 B   2 C   3 D Page 11

1   In the previous sentence, the author says that 42 new escalators are to be part of Central Station's upgrade. The missing sentence refers to the length and weight of nine of these escalators that are part of the upgrade: Nine of these escalators are 45 metres long and weigh more than 26 tonnes. The sentence that follows points out these particular escalators will be the longest in the Southern Hemisphere.

2   In the previous sentence, the author says the upgrade will include an underground pedestrian link. The missing sentence gives the length of this pedestrian link: This will be 80 metres long. The sentence that follows explains how pedestrians will use this link to connect with other modes of transport.

3   In the previous sentence, the author points out the complexity of the engineering involved in the upgrade. The missing sentence explains part of that complexity: Building has to be carried out beneath the surface as suburban trains run above. The sentence that follows suggests the outcome will make this worthwhile as the result will be a world-class resource.

The unused sentence is A.

1 A   2 A   3 B Page 14

1   The reader learns that the person Little Red Cap thinks is her grandmother is the wolf in disguise. Since the wolf has already eaten the grandmother, there is tension as to whether the wolf will also devour Little Red Cap.

Text B is incorrect. The tension is resolved by St George winning the battle.

2   The wolf uses lies and deceit to outwit Little Red Cap.

Text B is incorrect. The giant uses physical force against St George, not deceit.

3 Combat between the giant and St George is a drawn-out fight that lasts until noon.

Text A is incorrect. Combat between the wolf and the grandmother is over in an instant.

YEAR 3 THINKING SKILLS

PRACTICE QUESTIONS

1 A 2 C 3 C 4 B   Page 23

1 The text states that the Daintree rainforest is probably the oldest tropical rainforest in the world and that it is home to plants and animals that are not found anywhere else in the world. These statements support the main idea that 'The Daintree rainforest needs to be protected for the future'.

B and C are incorrect. These statements support the main idea.

D is incorrect. This statement provides a reason for the creator to be concerned that the Daintree rainforest might not be protected for the future.

2 **C is correct.** The text tells you the cook can use a mixture of fruits in the three-fruit salad but he always uses mango. You are also told that if there's no mango, the cook will use pineapple. However, the question says the cook will not use pineapple so you can assume mango is available. Along with mango, the other fruits to use will be banana and kiwi fruit.

A is incorrect. It's a three-fruit salad so there need to be two other fruits with the mango.

B is incorrect. It's a three-fruit salad so you need three fruits in the answer.

D is incorrect. The question tells you the cook is not using pineapple.

3 **C is correct.** If it is true that not everything you eat can be eaten by your dog, you need to find the statement that adds additional evidence to support this argument. Most humans can eat chocolate but it is toxic to dogs.

A is incorrect. This statement tells you which kinds of human food dogs can eat so it does not support the argument.

B and D are incorrect. These statements might be true but they don't support the argument that some human food is not healthy for dogs.

4 **B is correct.** Compare the statements of Letitia and Harry about the meaning of the sign to work out whose reasoning is correct. Harry uses correct reasoning to work out that the sign means any glass, not just bottles and glasses.

A is incorrect. Letitia is wrong to only look at the images of the bottle and the glass and state that jars are allowed in the pool area.

C is incorrect. Harry uses correct reasoning but Letitia does not.

D is incorrect. Harry uses correct reasoning.

1 B 2 A 3 B 4 B 5 D 6 C 7 A
8 C 9 A   Page 25

1 The differences between the numbers in the sequence are all 3. The next number will be 11 + 3 = 14.

2 Each number is half the one before. $\frac{1}{2}$ of 40 = 20.

3 As SEAT is X45Z, we know that S becomes X, E is 4, A is 5 and T is coded to Z. So TEA is Z45.

4 The point of the arrow is moving in a clockwise direction by 45° each time. The size of the arrow is alternating.

5 Each of the given shapes has only 1 line that is dotted. The first shape has 4 lines that are solid, the third shape has 2 solid lines and the fourth shape has 1 solid boundary. So the best fit for the missing shape would have 3 solid lines and 1 dotted line.

6 Work through the pattern. Each number is multiplied by 2 and then 2 is subtracted to get the next one. So 2 × 3 − 2 = 4; 2 × 4 − 2 = 6; 2 × 6 − 2 = 10. The first four numbers are 3, 4, 6 and 10.

7 Match the given words with their codes.

D	A	U	B	G	O	N	E
6	X	H	2	Z	9	8	V

So 2H6ZV can be easily read.

It is BUDGE.

8 You could write out the whole alphabet with its matching number but this is a long and time-consuming process. Z is the last of the 26 letters so it is 26. A = 1, B = 2 and E = 5 can be quickly worked out. The only tricky letter is R and counting through the alphabet we find it is 18.

9 Examining the 'bricks' in this wall looking for the pattern, we can see that the number in each brick is the sum of the two numbers below it. (28 + 31 = 59; 16 + 12 = 28; 11 + 5 = 16). So, continuing this pattern, 12 + 19 = 31; 5 + 7 = 12 and 7 + 12 = 19.

1 D **2** D **3** C **4** B **5** A   (Page 27)

1 This is a piece of logic. You are given two statements (called premises) and must draw a conclusion from them. The logic comes in from the words used: all, some, most. You cannot infer that, for instance, if all cats have 4 legs and some cats are black that most cats are black; or similarly if some cats like cream that most cats drink cream; or, again, if most cats purr that all cats will purr. D is, however, logical: all cats have 4 legs and most cats have tails (not, for instance, the Manx), then most cats will have 4 legs and a tail. The last part (after 'therefore') is called the conclusion.

2 Draw a picture or diagram:

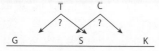

The clues given tell you Gary will be first (no-one is ahead of him), Karen will be last (no-one is behind her) and Sara is in the middle somewhere. The last clue tells you that Tina is behind Sara but ahead of Chris so Sara must be second.

3 The underwear and pyjamas are diagonally opposite each other so one of these is on the top and one on the bottom. The socks are on the top as well so the remaining drawer, holding the T-shirts, must be on the bottom. If the underwear is on the top, it will be on top of the T-shirts and beside the socks with the pyjamas on the bottom. However, the underwear could be on the bottom, meaning the pyjamas will be on the top, beside the socks, so none of the other options are the option that **must** be correct.

4 The Roses won the first game. If the Ferns won the second game, they won that game immediately after the Roses won a game. If the Roses won the second game, then the Ferns, who won the last game, won that game immediately after the Roses won a game. Or draw a diagram: the only possibilities are RFF or RRF.

5 Emily is next to both Patrick and Sarah so is in the room between them. The order must be Patrick, Emily, Sarah. Freya is not next to Harold. So Patrick, Emily and Sarah can't be in rooms 1, 2 and 3 or in rooms 3, 4 and 5. They must be in rooms 2, 3 and 4. Sarah must be in room 4. Freya is in a lower-numbered room than Harold so Freya must be in room 1. Harold must be in room 5, Patrick is in room 2 and Emily is in room 3.

1 D **2** C **3** D **4** C **5** A **6** A **7** A **8** D (Page 29)

1 Harvey spent $20.00 – $7.30 or $12.70 in total. Together the apples cost 6 × 70c or $4.20. The difference is the price of the watermelon: $12.70 – $4.20 = $8.50

2 Cora needed the $2 but another $2 would be too much to be the exact money. Two of the 50c pieces is another dollar, making $3. The only way to make up the remaining 65c is with another 50c piece, a 10c and a 5c (6 coins).

3   Trial and error is the best approach. $15 + 5 = 20$ but $15 - 5 = 10$, not 4. $11 + 7 = 18$ not 20. $16 + 4 = 20$ but $16 - 4 = 12$, not 4. $12 + 8 = 20$ and $12 - 8 = 4$.

4   Make sure your thinking is clear: How much did they have left? What they started with minus (–) their costs:
$1900 + $150 + $240 + $155 = $2445.

The total costs are $2445.

The amount left is $2500 – $2445 which is $55.

5   Make your list of costs and repayments. Costs should add up to $24.30; the repayment from the friend reduces the costs by $1.75 (take that from the costs), making $22.55. Then add the $2.45 which was left over to get $25.00.

6   The window cleaner begins on the middle rung. He goes up 3 rungs and down 5. So, then he is 2 rungs below the middle. Next, he goes up 7 rungs so is then 5 rungs above the middle rung. He then goes up another 6 rungs to the top, meaning the top rung of the ladder is 11 rungs above the middle.

There must also be 11 rungs below the middle rung. The ladder has $11 + 1 + 11$ or 23 rungs.

7   Work through each row or column as you can, remembering that they all add to 24. So the top number in the middle column must be 12. This means the last number in the top row must be 7. The bottom number in the last column must be 11 (using the diagonal $5 + 8 + 11 = 24$). So the middle number in the last column, X, must be 6 ($7 + 6 + 11 = 24$).

5	12	7
10	8	6
9	4	11

8   From Alice, Mabel must pay $7 for each mug. $12 \times 7 = 84$ so Mabel would need to pay $84 for the set of 12.

Max has an offer to 'buy 2 get 1 free'. Each mug costs $10 so 2 mugs will cost $20. The

third mug is then free so Mabel can get 3 mugs for $20. $4 \times 3 = 12$ so if Mabel buys 4 lots of 3 mugs, she will have 12. The cost of 12 mugs is $4 \times 20 or $80.

Penny has an offer to 'buy 3 get 1 free'. Each of Penny's mugs costs $9 so 3 mugs will cost $3 \times 9 or $27. The fourth mug is then free so Mabel can get 4 mugs for $27. As $3 \times 4 = 12$, if Mabel buys 3 lots of 4 mugs, she will have 12. The cost of 12 mugs is $3 \times 27 or $81.

From Thomas, Mabel can buy 2 mugs for $2 \times 8 or $16. She can then buy a third mug for half the price. As half of 8 is 4, Mabel can buy 3 mugs for $16 + $4 or $20. She can buy 12 mugs for $4 \times 20 or $80.

Mabel can buy 12 mugs for the least amount from either Max or Thomas.

YEAR 3 MATHEMATICAL REASONING

PRACTICE QUESTIONS

1 A **2** D **3** D **4** D **5** C **6** C   Page 31

1   A mirror image must be exactly the same but reversed; the same colours in the same positions but on the other side.

2   Imagine the shape reflected across a vertical line.

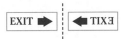

Fold the paper along the dotted line and view from the other side.

3   You can't take scissors into the test, otherwise you could cut the shapes up and try them on the shaded one. Try doing this in your mind.

4   There are 8 small squares and 3 larger ones.

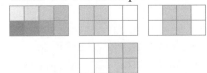

5 Again try to imagine you have the smaller shape and try to fit it into the larger one with your eyes. Don't forget it can be turned round. For each 6 cubes you will be able to fit it (the 3-cube figure) in twice. There are 18 cubes in the large shape so your answer will be 6.

6 When the net is folded the 6 will be opposite 3, 4 will be opposite 2 and 1 opposite 5. As 6 + 3 = 9, the answer is 9. Practise cutting out and folding nets.

1 A **2** B **3** C **4** E **5** B **6** D **7** C **8** D   Page 33

1 Potatoes cost 2 × $2.50 or $5. The carrots cost 2 × $1.50 or $3 and the rockmelons are the same. So the total cost is $5 + $3 + $3 or $11 and the change is $15 – $11 or $4. Alternatively add the three unit costs and then multiply by 2 to get the total cost.

2 Read carefully and match the working to the question. The cost to go in is $5.00. Mary has to pay that amount but her three brothers can go for half of that price. So Mary must pay $5.00 (for herself) + $\frac{1}{2}$ of $5.00 for each of her 3 brothers ($5.00 + 3 × $\frac{1}{2}$ × $5.00).

3 Seven hundreds more than 82 569 is 82 569 + 700 or 83 269.

4 Read the question carefully and look for the important information. Here we are told that Ken is 9. He is one year older than Peter so Peter is 8. Peter is twice as old as Marco so Marco is 4.

5 The 'number of 100s in' is the same as 'divided by (÷) 100'; the 'number of 1000s in' is the same as '÷ 1000', and so on. So, 4000 ÷ 100 gives the number of hundreds in 4000. (There are 40.)

6 Imogen has twice as many as Vincent so Vincent has one share and Imogen has two. There are three shares altogether so each share

is 24 ÷ 3 or 8. So Vincent has 8 marbles and Imogen has 2 × 8 or 16. (Check: 8 + 16 = 24.)

7 Consider each rectangle: X is divided into 5 parts and 3 parts are shaded. So $\frac{3}{5}$ is shaded. Y is divided into 10 parts and 6 of those are shaded. So $\frac{6}{10}$ or $\frac{3}{5}$ is shaded. Imagine the two parts on the top right moved so that the first three of the five columns are shaded. Z is divided into 8 parts and 3 of those are shaded. So $\frac{3}{8}$ is shaded, not $\frac{3}{5}$. Only X and Y have $\frac{3}{5}$ shaded.

8 For every 4 black tiles there are 3 white ones. 28 ÷ 4 = 7, meaning there are 7 rows. Each row has 3 white tiles. 7 × 3 = 21, meaning there are 21 white tiles altogether.

1 B **2** A **3** B **4** A **5** D   Page 35

1 The design has four pieces that are all the same so we only need worry about one piece. Imagine the grid that covers the design and count the squares, matching halves. Each of the four pieces has $4\frac{1}{2}$ squares shaded. 4 lots of $4\frac{1}{2}$ is 4 lots of 4 + 4 halves = 16 + 2 = 18.

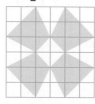

2 Each square has side length 10 m. Rachel will be 10 m from the starting point when she finishes the instructions.

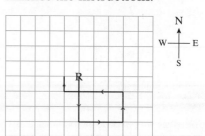

3 There are 10 marks on the jug so each mark is (1000 ÷ 10) mL or 100 mL. So the jug has 600 mL of milk. 600 – 350 = 250 so Sophie will have 250 mL left in the jug.

4   The top is 8 m long so the whole bottom must also be 8 m long. The right side is 6 m long so the whole left side must be 6 m long.
8 + 8 + 6 + 6 = 28

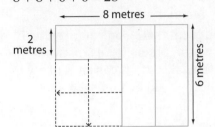

5   Sharma ran $1\frac{1}{2}$ km altogether. 1 km is 1000 m so $1\frac{1}{2}$ km is 1500 m. Straightaway we can see that together 200 m and 800 m is 1000 m or 1 km. 400 m + 75 m leaves just 25 m for the three-legged race.

1 A **2** C **3** C **4** B **5** E **6** E **7** B **8** D   Page 37

1   15 minutes is $\frac{1}{4}$ of an hour. Sally must be home $3\frac{3}{4}$ hours later. $\frac{3}{4}$ hour later is 12:30 and another 3 hours after that is 3:30 pm.

2   If it is 10 am in New Zealand, it will be 8 am in Sydney. If it is 8 am in Sydney, it will be 6 am in Perth.

3   Use your number line and go back the 7 hours to midnight, then another 3 hours back (to make the 10 hours behind) takes us to 9 pm the night before.

4   A diagram: 7 March is a Tuesday so hop by a week at a time and 14 March is a Tuesday, 21 March is a Tuesday and 28 March is a Tuesday. Another 3 days till the end of March (remember it is a 31-day month) + 4 days in April gives you exactly another 7 days to 4 April so it will be a Tuesday.

5   Again, a diagram or clocks would be useful. Remember in your thinking that Friday 6:30 pm to Saturday 6:30 pm is 24 hours, and there is another 24 hours (making 48 hours) to Sunday 6:30 pm, then add 12 hours to 6:30

Monday morning (6:30 am) and add the one hour to 7:30 am Monday.

6   Do your time line—add the 30 minutes first, which takes the time to 11:00 am, then add the 7 hours and it takes you through to 6:00 pm. With questions like this, it is always easier if you can work using full hours, from 10 o'clock or 11 o'clock etc to keep the process simple.

7   The opera is performed 4 times each week. 4 weeks is 4 × 7 days, or 28 days. The opera will be performed 4 × 4 = 16 times up until 28 June. It will then be performed on the nights of Friday 29 June and Saturday 30 June. The opera will be performed 18 times.

8   Keith travels for an hour on each of 5 days so that is 5 hours altogether. 30 minutes is $\frac{1}{2}$ hour. So Keith spends $5\frac{1}{2}$ hours travelling during the week.

1 D **2** D **3** C   Page 39

1   Use your ruler if it's hard to line up the columns and the numbers. The first two columns are the people we must count (before 6 am and 6–7 am). 10 + 25 = 35.

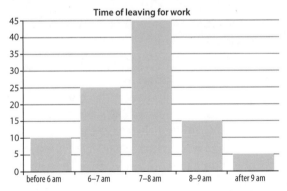

2   Thirty fruit were sold, which is double the sale of rolls (15).

3   Check the chart with the graph and you will find that softball should be 50, not 40 as represented by the bar on the graph.

YEAR 3 READING SAMPLE TEST Page 40

1 C 2 A 3 B 4 D 5 C 6 D 7 A 8 C 9 A
10 E 11 A 12 C 13 B 14 D 15 D 16 A 17 B
18 C 19 B 20 D

1   It is clear the king is enormously wealthy. You can work out that this is the most likely reason for her to marry him.

    A is incorrect. If she had loved the king, she would not have treated his children in the cruel way she does.

    B is incorrect. She has no interest in being a stepmother and, in fact, got rid of all the children.

    D is incorrect. Although the king may have had a good reputation, her evil ways suggest this would be of less interest to her than his wealth.

2   You can judge that it is the queen's lies that convince the king his sons are not the good men he thought them. After this, he decides to stop troubling himself about them.

    B is incorrect. He didn't know his sons had been turned into swans and there is no evidence he saw them fly away.

    C is incorrect. There is no mention of him being jealous of them.

    D is incorrect. Although he may have preferred Eliza, this is not stated and it would not be a reason to stop caring for his sons.

3   Eliza and her brothers were close to each other before the arrival of the queen. When her brothers are turned into swans and banished from their home, they hover over the cottage where their sister had been sent to live. You can work out they were hoping to attract her attention.

    The other options are incorrect. There is no suggestion the swans were looking for rest, had a message for the peasant and his wife, or were looking for food.

4   Animals do turn into other things in fairytales (like frogs into princes) but it is unusual for animals to turn into flowers as the toads do.

The other options are incorrect. Wicked stepmothers (like Snow White), great forests (in most fairytales) and obedient children being badly treated (like Hansel and Gretel) are all very familiar motifs.

5   The general truth that good will overcome evil is a powerful predictor of what will happen in this tale. This means it is likely the queen's evil ways will be punished and happiness restored.

    A is incorrect. The queen is quite clever. Even so, not being very clever is not usually a quality that gets punished in fairytales.

    B is incorrect. The Queen does not have a fairy godmother but even if she did, it would be unlikely to be enough to save her in a fairytale setting.

    D is incorrect. Although good characters in fairytales sometimes seek revenge, this seems unlikely in Eliza's case.

6   Stanza two gives the daughter's words and reports what she says to her mother; stanza four reports what the daughter thinks and what she says to her mother.

    A is incorrect. The mother's words are given in stanza one.

    B and C are incorrect. The mother's thoughts are given in stanza three.

7   The daughter persistently uses reasoned argument to get her mother to allow her to play in the park.

    B and C are incorrect. Although her words 'I'd rather play now' could be seen as cheeky, they are not rude or unpleasant, especially as she follows that comment with a 'Please let me, okay?'

    D is incorrect. Although she is mostly polite, she relies more on using reason to persuade her mother to allow her to do what she wants to do.

8   When the mother begins to think how quickly time passes, she wonders if she has given her daughter the right answer; she begins to change her mind.

A is incorrect. The mother is not as influenced by her daughter's pleas as by her own thoughts.

B and D are incorrect. The mother is willing to refuse at first and this implies she is not afraid of her daughter's anger.

9   Once the mother has thought about how quickly time passes, she seems very likely to change her mind and let her daughter play in the park. The daughter puts these thoughts in a convincing way (just yesterday/today was tomorrow) making it seem highly likely she has won the argument.

B and D are incorrect. By the end of the poem it seems much more likely the daughter will be allowed to play in the park than that her mother will refuse her request.

C is incorrect. It is not absolutely certain the daughter has won the argument. It is implied that the answer to her question probably will be agreement but this agreement is not yet stated.

10 In the previous sentence the author is talking about a sighting of the Loch Ness Monster mentioned in St Columba's biography. This sentence gives more detail about what St Columba actually saw. The sentence that follows explains how St Columba reacted to this sight, what he said and what the Monster did.

11 In the previous sentence the author says that, occasionally, people have made claims they have seen the Monster in the Loch. This sentence gives a specific example of a sighting reported in the *Inverness Courier* in 1933. The sentence that follows refers to another sighting that took place soon after.

12 In the previous sentence the author reports that *The Daily Mail* hired a game hunter to capture Nessie. This sentence tells that the hired man found footprints he thought might be the Monster's. The sentence that follows explains that the footprints were proved to be part of a hoax.

13 In the previous sentence the author is talking about how people continue to have theories about the Monster's existence. This sentence refers to a photo that led some to believe it was a survivor from the dinosaur family. The sentence that follows suggests some particular dinosaur families to whom Nessie may be related.

14 In the previous sentence the author is talking about how scientists have done experiments in the Loch to try to find out if the Monster exists. This sentence states that they have not yet found evidence of this. The sentence following explains that, on the other hand, they have come across underwater objects they can't explain!

The unused sentence is F.

15 The author explains that funnel web spiders build funnel shaped webs so you can assume this is a spider whose name reflects the shape of its web.

The other options are incorrect. None of the spiders referred to in these texts have names that reflect their web shapes.

16 In this story Arachne is boastful and her pride leads her to behave in ways that are punished by the Goddess Athena. She is changed from a weaver of tapestries into a hairy spider!

The other options are incorrect. None of these texts illustrate this saying.

17 This text includes the information that some spiders are able to travel long distances by catching the wind with their silken threads, a process known as ballooning.

B is incorrect because, although it refers to the unusual way a daddy long legs moves if it loses a leg, it doesn't use this method to travel long distances.

A and D are incorrect. They do not refer to spiders' ways of travelling long distances.

18 The legend that good luck follows the sighting of a daddy long legs in the evening is mentioned in this text.

B and D are incorrect. They do not refer to legends.

A is incorrect. The Arachne story is a myth (not based on fact) rather than a legend (usually based on fact but exaggerated over time.)

19 General information about history, body parts and the behaviours of spiders are provided in this text.

C and D are incorrect. They are about specific types of spider, the daddy long legs and the funnel web.

A is incorrect. It is about a mythical spider.

20 The male funnel web spider is said to be more lightly built than the female.

The other options are incorrect. They do not include comparisons between males and females.

YEAR 3 THINKING SKILLS SAMPLE TEST   Page 46

1 D 2 A 3 D 4 C 5 D 6 A 7 D 8 D 9 C
10 C 11 C 12 B 13 A 14 B 15 C 16 A 17 B
18 C 19 B 20 B

1 Every element will be seen in reverse. Imagine the reflection.

2 Owen uses correct reasoning when he says he thinks the animal might be a donkey because it has three features that indicate this to be true: a short mane, a tail like a cow and big ears. He is not certain so he says 'I think …', leaving open the possibility that it might not be a donkey. Amar is wrong to state the baby must be a mule. The text tells you mules are only born to female horses and not donkeys.

3 Find the difference between the first and second test marks for each boy. This difference is 5 for Abraham, 4 for James, 6 for Paul and 7 for Thomas. So Thomas improved the most.

4 If it usually takes a month to master the three-ball cascade, it could take some people more than a month and some people less than a month.

5 The third row has 0, 4, 5 and 6 so the missing domino can only have 1, 2 or 3. The fourth

column has 0, 2, 3, 5 and 6 so the missing half of the domino can only have 1 or 4. It must be 1. The fifth column has 1, 2, 4, 5 and 6 so the missing half of the domino can only have 0 or 3. It must be 3.

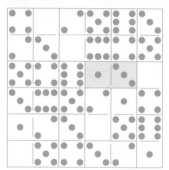

6

7 The argument is that Karim will succeed faster than most and become a professional drummer in spite of this taking years of practice and requiring excellent coordination. Any information that undermines the argument will weaken it: in this case the fact that Karim has poor coordination could hinder his ability to become a professional drummer in a shorter time than most.

8 Leon did not consider that some of the residents who own an electric wheelchair might have left their wheelchairs behind and left the home by a different means.

9 There are performances on 3 nights each week. If 6 January is a Thursday, then so is 13 January, 20 January and 27 January. There are 3 weeks of performances beginning on the 7th, 13th and 20th. This means 3 × 3 or 9 performances. There are also performances on 27 January and 28 January and two Sunday afternoon performances. So there will be 13 performances altogether.

10 Since everyone had to vote for two poems and, knowing that no-one voted for either 'Jim who was eaten by a lion' or 'Triantiwontigongolope', you can work out which poem won. All students must have voted for 'The owl and the pussycat' by either

voting for 'The owl and the pussycat' plus 'Triantiwontigongolope' or by voting for 'The owl and the pussycat' plus 'Jim who was eaten by a lion'.

The other options are incorrect. They don't help you work out which poem won the vote.

11 When folded, if the face with the star is on the right side and the lightning at the top then the heart will be at the back. The face with the circle will then be on the left side, the square will be on the bottom and the triangle at the front. The square will be opposite the lightning, the triangle opposite the heart and the circle opposite the star.

12 Alice is directly opposite Ilona so there are two people between them on each side of the table. Nadine is next to Hannah so they are the two people on one side. Maisie and Erica must therefore be the two people on the other side. Maisie must be next to Erica. Erica might be next to Alice but she might also be next to Ilona and not Alice. Nadine cannot be next to Maisie as she is between Hannah and either Alice or Ilona. Ilona might or might not be next to Hannah.

13 The argument is that the dinosaur would have been fierce in battle because of its club-like tail so any further evidence to support the idea that the tail was used as a weapon strengthens the argument. Sharp blades along the sides of the tail increased the tail's effectiveness in battle.

14 Braiden is correct when he says if Yoda gets diarrhoea tomorrow, he won't be allowed in the car. We know this is true from the information in the box. Dean's reasoning is incorrect. We know Yoda digs holes in the lawn when he's not allowed in the car but he might dig holes in the lawn at other times too. Therefore Dean can't say for certain that Yoda had diarrhoea yesterday just because he dug holes.

15 Keshia must choose shapes from each box but none of parallelogram, pentagon, triangle or octagon comes from Box 1. So Keshia cannot have chosen those four shapes. Keshia could

have chosen circle from Box 1, triangle from Box 2, square from Box 3 and kite from Box 4. So she could have chosen the shapes in A. Keshia could have chosen circle from Box 1, rectangle from Box 2, octagon from Box 3 and pentagon from Box 4. So she could have chosen the shapes in B. Keshia could have chosen kite from Box 1, hexagon from Box 2, pentagon from Box 3 and rectangle from Box 4. So she could have chosen the shapes in D.

16 If the second jellybean Ingrid ate was orange, then she ate that orange one after a red one. If the second jellybean was red, then the last jellybean Ingrid ate which was orange was eaten after a red one. So whatever colour the second jellybean was, Ingrid ate an orange one after a red one. The jellybeans could have been either 2 red and 1 orange or 1 orange and 2 red. So A and B are not the options that **must** have been correct. Ingrid cannot have eaten a red jellybean after an orange one so C is not correct.

17 The main idea the creator of the text wants you to accept is that the January 2022 eruption of the Hunga Tonga Hunga Ha'apai volcano in Tonga was a massive event. The rest of the text provides information about the eruption and therefore supports this main idea.

18 If Scarlet is not one of the reserves on Friday, then Marty must be available to be reserve. Since Marty is available, Niklas must also be a reserve and not Seiya. So Marty and Niklas will be travelling on the bus as debating team reserves on Friday.

A is incorrect. You are told that if Marty can be a reserve, then Niklas will go too.

B is incorrect. If Marty is going, then Niklas will go instead of Seiya.

D is incorrect. Niklas and Seiya cannot both go. Niklas will go on the bus instead of Seiya.

19 P1 cannot have Charlie (already in column P) or Ezekiel and Ivy (already in diagonal P1–S4). So P1 must be Lola. Charlie must be in Q2 completing the diagonal. In row 4, Ivy is not in P4 or S4 and cannot be in R4

because she is in R3, so Ivy must be in Q4. Q1 cannot be Ivy (Q4), Charlie (Q2) or Lola (P1) so Ezekiel's photo must be in Q1.

4	C	I	L	E
3	E	L	I	C
2	I	C	E	L
1	L	E	C	I
	P	Q	R	S

20 The main idea the creator of the text wants you to accept is that beehives are very busy. This is stated at the beginning of the text and reinforced in the conclusion. The rest of the text gives more information about how many bees live in a hive and the different activities within a hive, which all supports this main idea.

YEAR 3 MATHEMATICAL REASONING
SAMPLE TEST   Page 52

1 A 2 C 3 C 4 D 5 A 6 B 7 A 8 B 9 D
10 C 11 B 12 E 13 D 14 B 15 A 16 E 17 D
18 E 19 C 20 E

1 Sally spent $4.50 + $5.55 + $6.00 or a total of $16.05. She had $20 to start with so the amount she had left was $20.00 − $16.05 or $3.95.

2 Each shape needs to be imagined turned around 180° (not flipped). So if 1 was turned around, the dark blue square would be in the bottom-right corner like in 5 but the lightest blue would be at the middle top, not the mid-blue one. So both 1 and 5 can be discounted. 3 must be one of the shapes and if it turned around, the dark blue square would be in the top right and the mid-blue square in the middle of the bottom row. So it would be the same as shape 4. Turn the book around to see!

3 Eight hundreds more than 37 519 is 37 519 + 800 which is 38 319.

4 Each of the rectangles needs to be considered. X has 3 parts shaded out of 7 parts. The amount shaded is $\frac{3}{7}$ not $\frac{3}{4}$. Y has

5 parts shaded out of 6 parts but all the parts are not the same size. If a line is drawn down the middle, it divides the rectangle into 8 equal parts and 6 of those are shaded. As 6 out of 8 means 3 out of 4, Y has $\frac{3}{4}$ shaded. Z also has 6 equal parts shaded out of 8. Z has $\frac{3}{4}$ shaded.

5 Each square has side length 10 m. Imagine (or draw) the path that Ed would take. Ed finishes 10 m from his starting point.

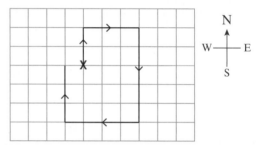

6 Imagine or shade the other half of the design. U1, W3, X5 and Y6 will all be shaded but V4 will not.

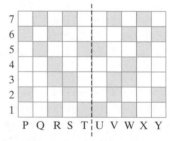

7 Twenty minutes to one in the afternoon is 12:40 pm. From 11:25 am until 12:25 pm is 1 hour. From 12:25 until 12:40 is 15 minutes. Pat was on the bus for 1 hour and 15 minutes.

8 The fence has 12 palings. If three out of four are painted, that will be 9 out of 12. Jess needs to paint another 6. Imagine the fence divided into groups of 4, with 3 of those 4 painted.

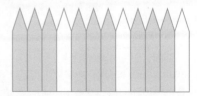

9 Ayesha found 2 parts and Jake found 1. So that is 3 parts altogether. $36 \div 3 = 12$ so each part is 12 shells. Jack found 12 shells and Ayesha found 2×12 or 24.

10 From 9 am until 12 noon is 3 hours and from 12 noon until 4 pm is 4 hours. So Modena works 3 hours on 3 days and 4 hours on 2 days. The hours are found by multiplying 3 by 3 and 4 by 2.

11 First find $94 - 17$. It is 77. So $58 + \blacklozenge = 77$. Subtracting 58 from both sides gives $\blacklozenge = 19$.

12 First work out the scale on both jugs. Each smaller mark must be 0.5 L on both. The smaller jug currently has 1.5 L and the larger jug has 3.5 L. 0.5 L is needed to fill the smaller jug. The larger jug will have 0.5 L less than 3.5 L. It will have 3 L.

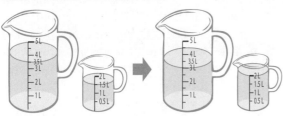

13 A packet of 6 is cheaper than 6 single rolls so Nigel needs to buy one packet of 6 and 4 single rolls. The lowest price he can pay is $\$2.00 + 4 \times \$0.40$ or $\$3.60$.

14 Cody will see 7 faces on 4 sides and 1 face at either end. $4 \times 7 + 2 = 28 + 2 = 30$

15 Consider each statement. The spinner has equal chances of stopping on 2 or 3 so statement 1 is correct. There are 2 numbers greater than 3 (4 and 5) and 2 numbers less than 3 (1 and 2). So James is equally likely to spin a number greater than 3 than a number less than 3. Statement 2 is not correct. There are 3 odd numbers (1, 3 and 5) and 2 even numbers (2 and 4). So James is more likely to spin an odd number than an even number. Statement 3 is not correct. So only statement 1 is correct.

16 Imagine, or draw, the possible cuts.

17 The numbers are going up by 3 each time. So the sequence is: 2, 5, 8, 11, 14, 17, 20, 23, 26, 29… The seventh term is 20 and the tenth term is 29. $20 + 29 = 49$

18 Each line on the vertical axis must represent 2 families. Now consider each statement. 3 families had 5 children and 1 family had 6 children so 4 families had either 5 or 6 children but 12 families had no children. Statement X is not correct. 32 families had 1 child, 48 had 2 children and 24 had 3 children. $32 + 48 + 24 = 104$ so statement Y is correct. 16 families had 4 children. $3 \times 16 = 6 \times 8 = 48$, the number that had 2 children. So statement Z is correct.

19 North is not pointing in the 'usual direction' so south-east is not below Zak's position. Draw the points of the compass on the diagram or turn the whole diagram to 'face the right way'. Haseeb can only be at T5.

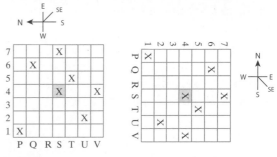

20 Counting the squares to find the perimeter, Billy's original shape has perimeter 14 cm. Shapes P and Q have perimeter 16 cm. Shapes R and S have perimeter 18 cm. In P and Q, two of the sides of the added squares just replace sides of the original shape; they are not extra.

YEAR 4 READING

PRACTICE QUESTIONS

1 D 2 A Page 59

1   **A and C are incorrect.** It is clear the Astute Fish has a complicated plan to outwit the Whale that involves swimming to a particular location. The Fish gives precise directions to make sure the Whale reaches that destination.

   B is incorrect. There is no evidence as to whether it is an easy swim or not.

2   The flattering words 'Noble and generous Cetacean' are used by the Astute Fish to gain the Whale's attention.

   B is incorrect. While it is true the Fish promises the Whale access to food, this is not how it first catches the Whale's attention.

   C is incorrect. The Fish keeps out of sight in order to keep out of harm's way, not to catch the Whale's attention.

   D is incorrect. The Fish offers practical advice to the Whale instead of showing it sympathy. It is, of course, entirely unsympathetic to the Whale who eats all the fish in the sea!

1 B 2 B Page 62

1   **A and C are incorrect.** Andy is seen as someone who works hard, inspires his community and brings cheerfulness to those he works with.

   D is incorrect. Although it is true the narrator approves of Andy, his feelings are stronger than approval: he admires everything about him.

2   Those who Andy leaves behind feel in low spirits and irritable, as if all is not as it should be.

   A is incorrect. There is nothing physically wrong with their hearts.

   C and D are incorrect. Although things are said to be dull and depressing without Andy, this is not as extreme as being full of misery or having hearts that are broken.

1 C 2 A 3 D Page 65

1   The previous question asks what makes Vale Street special. The missing sentence answers that question: It is thought to be the steepest street in England. The sentence that follows confirms the challenges presented by its steepness to those who try to get from the bottom to the top.

2   The previous sentence asks how people park their cars in this street. The missing sentence answers this question: They park them perpendicular to the road. The sentence that follows explains that otherwise the cars can be in danger of rolling down the hill.

3   The previous sentence explains how the residents of Vale Street use the steepness of their street to have an Easter egg-rolling competition. The missing sentence points out that Vale Street is not the only steep street in the world. The sentence that follows claims that even though there are other steep streets, it is only in Vale Street that an Easter egg-rolling competition is held.

The unused sentence is B.

1 A 2 A 3 B Page 68

1   John Parkes marries and has twelve children. He earns a living to support the family by setting up camp and working as a sawyer.

   B is incorrect. Although Pu Yi married several times, he does not have children and moves away from his own family to live in a different society.

2   John Parkes is honoured by his local community with a memorial after his death to indicate its respect for him.

   B is incorrect. Pu Yi holds important positions in society but these seem more a matter of his birth into a royal family rather than respect for his achievements at a local level.

3   Pu Yi is well connected, fills important leadership roles and is likely to have received a good education. The fact that he writes a

book which is then used as a basis for a film implies he has well developed literacy skills.

A is incorrect. John Parkes was already working as a nailor at the age of six. His history does not suggest there was ever time for schooling and education.

YEAR 4 THINKING SKILLS
PRACTICE QUESTIONS

1 D **2** A **3** C **4** B   `Page 77`

1 Pinata and sleepover are both included in the list of things Dora would like but neither Jim nor Lily mentions either one.

A is incorrect. Dora wants tacos and a pinata but Lily would also like tacos.

B is incorrect. Dora wants a sleepover and cake but both Jim and Lily would also like cake.

C is incorrect. Dora doesn't say she wants laser tag or a disco.

2 Sam's conclusion is that there is nothing wrong with talking during the test. He based this conclusion on the evidence that everyone else was talking. So for his conclusion to hold, it must be assumed that it is okay do something if everyone else is doing it.

B is incorrect. This is Sam's conclusion not his assumption.

C is incorrect. This assumption does not support Sam's conclusion that there is nothing wrong with talking during a test.

D is incorrect. This is the evidence Sam based his conclusion on.

3 The statement—that an environmental study shows an extension will destroy the beach—supports the coastal engineer's claim that the wall should not be extended because the existing wall is already causing erosion from which the beach may never recover.

A is incorrect. This statement about an alternative to a vertical wall could add to the engineer's argument. However, it doesn't offer the best support for the claim about the wall causing damage to the beach.

B is incorrect. This statement does not support the coastal engineer's claim.

D is incorrect. Rather than supporting the engineer's claim, this statement supports an argument in favour of the wall.

4 Only Sara's reasoning is correct. We know that only players who attended every training session during the season will be allowed to play in the exhibition match. Since Sara missed a session she will not be allowed to play.

A is incorrect. Even though Ethan attended every training session, there may be other reasons why some players are unable to play in the special match. So it is a flaw in his reasoning to say he will **definitely** be playing.

The other options are incorrect by a process of elimination.

1 C **2** C **3** B **4** D **5** B **6** A **7** B
8 C **9** D   `Page 79`

1 In this particular question, direction, size and shade change so there are three elements in the sequence to keep in mind.

The point of the arrow is moving in order in a clockwise direction by 45° (half a right angle) at a time. Another way of looking at it would be that the sequence is moving around the points of the compass, beginning west → north-west → north → north-east → east → south-east → south. Following this sequence, the next direction will be south-west.

The first arrow is much larger than the second and the pattern can be seen to be large-small-large-small, and so on, alternating. The last arrow in the series is large so the arrow in question must be small.

The first arrow is white in the centre, the second is blue, and so on, alternating. The last arrow is white so the next must be blue.

Thus the answer must be the arrow which is small, pointing to the south-west and blue.

2 Find the differences between the terms:

1	2	4	7	**?**	16	22	29
1	2	3	**?**	**?**	6	7	

The differences between the numbers seem to be increasing by 1 each time. So the two missing differences would be 4 and 5. 7 + 4 = 11 and 11 + 5 = 16. This fits the sequence so the missing number must be 11.

3 This is tricky. The series goes forwards then backwards, making two series within one:

13 9 18 14 28 24
\ / \ / \ / \ / \
−4 +9 −4 +14 −4 ?
−4 ×2 −4 ×2 −4 ?

The minus four (−4) is obvious but the other series is less so. Next try multiplying instead of adding. This makes it clearer; the next step will be multiplying by 2. 24 × 2 = 48.

4 Look for repeated numbers in the code: There are three 6s in positions two, six and ten; two 3s in positions three and seven; and two 7s in positions four and eight. This means that the same letter must be in those positions. Only D has the same letter repeated in positions two, six and ten (it is an 'o'); then another letter repeated in positions three and seven (it is an 'm'); and again, in positions four and eight (this time, it is an 'e'). The message is 'Come home now'.

5 Work through the sequence following the rule. The first number is 80. Half of 80 is 40 and 8 more is 48. So the second number is 48. Half of 48 is 24. The third number is 24 + 8 or 32. Half of 32 is 16 so the fourth number is 16 + 8 or 24. Half of 24 is 12 so the fifth number is 12 + 8 or 20.

6 From the given words we can see that the code for A is 1, B is 2, C is 3, E is 5 and G is 7. Each letter is being replaced by its position in the alphabet. D is the 4th letter and H is the 8th letter. HEAD will be 8514.

7 This code numbers the letters as they appear (with repeated letters being given the same number as before). AGAINST only has one repeated letter. It will be 1213456.

8 The pattern tells us the two numbers beneath each number multiply to it. So 10 × P = 200, meaning P must be 20. P × Q = 240 and, if P is 20, Q must be 12. T × 3 = 12 so T must be 4.

S × T = P which means that S × 4 = 20 and so S is 5. S + T = 5 + 4.

9 The total fine is the sum of the fines for each day. Those fines are doubling each time. So the amount, in cents, for the first 7 days will be 1 + 2 + 4 + 8 + 16 + 32 + 64. That is a total of 127 cents or $1.27.

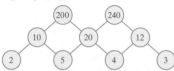

1 A 2 D 3 B 4 C 5 D   Page 81

1 Jennifer, Ezra and Kate are all behind Ashleigh so she must be either first or second. But Ashleigh is behind Martin. So Ashleigh is second in line. Martin must be first in the queue. Jennifer must be either the third or fourth person and Ezra must be either fourth or fifth. Kate could be the third, fourth or fifth.

2 Sally is to the left of Ava so Ava is right of Sally. Tiffany is also to the right of Sally. Ellen is to the right of Tiffany so she is also right of Sally. As Ava, Tiffany and Ellen are all right of Sally, Sally must be furthest left. Tiffany cannot be furthest left because she is to the right of Sally. Either Ellen or Ava will be furthest right but there is not enough information to say which statement **must** be true.

3 Olivia is sitting next to Noah. So Tahlia must be next to Zeb. Tahlia is diagonally opposite Olivia so Zeb must be directly opposite Olivia. There is no information about which two are closer to the beach or to the road. So options A and D are not options that **must** be correct. As Zeb is facing the river, Tahlia must also be facing the river so option C is not correct.

4 Mo is one of the placegetters. Mo only appears in week 3 so he must be the week 3 winner. Caleb also only appears in week 3. He cannot be a winner from any of the weeks so cannot be a placegetter in week 5. The winners could be James from week 1, Oliver

from week 2, Mo from week 3 and Alex from week 4. So Alex could be a week 5 placegetter. The winners could be Billy from week 1, Oliver from week 2, Mo from week 3 and James from week 4. So Billy could be a week 5 placegetter. The winners could be Max from week 1, Oliver from week 2, Mo from week 3 and James from week 4. So Max could be a week 5 placegetter.

5   As Madison and Vanessa live furthest apart, they must live in the two end houses. Dana lives next to Madison so cannot live next to Vanessa. The two women between Dana and Laura must be Jessica and Abigail. So Laura must live next door to Vanessa.

Madison	Dana	Jessica	Abigail	Laura	Vanessa

1 D **2** C **3** C **4** B **5** D   Page 84

1   If the second rose Pippa planted was white, then she planted that white one straight after the pink one she planted first. If the second rose was pink, then the last rose Pippa planted, which was white, was planted straight after that pink one. So whatever colour the second rose was, Pippa must have planted a white one straight after a pink one. The roses could have been either 2 pink and 1 white or 1 white and 2 pink. A and B are not the options that **must** have been correct. Pippa cannot have planted a pink rose after a white one so C is not correct.

2   We know Celine's mark was lower than Oliver's, Hugo's and Abigail's but it might have been higher than Archie's or Charlotte's. So Celine might not have come last. Hugo and Abigail got the same mark. This mark was higher than that of Charlotte, Archie and Celine but lower than Oliver's. So Oliver must have got the highest mark and Hugo and Abigail came equal second. Archie's mark was lower than Charlotte's, which was lower than that of Abigail and Hugo. So Archie did get a lower mark than Hugo. A, B and D are all true statements so they cannot be the correct answer.

3   The sports that Matilda can choose from in term 3 are soccer, netball and hockey. The only one of these that Matilda has chosen is netball so netball must be the sport chosen in term 3. Matilda could have chosen softball in term 2, tennis in term 4 and cricket in term 1. So A, B and D are not correct.

4   Amelia is older than Tia but younger than Daisy. So Daisy is older than both Amelia and Tia. Layla is younger than Daisy so Daisy is also older than Layla. Daisy must be the oldest. A, C and D might be true but we don't know they **must** be true. Tia is younger than both Amelia and Daisy but she might or might not be younger than Layla. Layla is younger than Daisy but there is no other information about her. She might or might not be the youngest. Amelia is younger than Daisy and older than Tia so she might be the second oldest but she might also be the second youngest.

5   There are 3 green and 4 red marbles so together there are 7 green or red marbles. The rest of the 11 marbles are blue so 4 must be blue. Now consider each statement. As there are the same number of red and blue marbles, Hayden is equally likely to take red or blue. Statement 1 is correct. There are more blue marbles than green so Hayden is more likely to take a blue than a green. Statement 2 is correct. There are fewer green marbles than red ones so Hayden is less likely to take a green than a red. Statement 3 is correct.

YEAR 4 MATHEMATICAL REASONING

PRACTICE QUESTIONS

1 D **2** C **3** E **4** D **5** E **6** A **7** B   Page 86

1   This is a matter of mentally fitting the shapes into the shaded figure. You have three parts (quarters) of a circle and the fourth part has been taken over by the rectangle.

2 This tests your spatial skills—your ability to picture objects in space. Again, try to 'fit' the small shape into the large one. Your solution plan should involve counting the squares, both the ones you can see and those you can't. The small shape will fit into the large one 6 times.

3 There are 8 small triangles, 4 triangles covering 2 smaller ones each and another 4 covering 4 smaller ones each.

4 The four corner cubes will have paint on 4 faces. The other 6 cubes will have paint on 3 faces (front, back and top of the top row and front, back and bottom of the bottom row).

5 If 3 is at the top and 1 is at the front, then 5 will be next to both of those on the right side. 2 will be on the left side, 4 on the bottom and 6 at the back. So the sum of the numbers on the right side and back is 5 + 6, or 11.

6 Imagine the shape flipped over a vertical line.

7 From the front view we can see the book that is furthest left is dark blue so the answer can only be A or B. From the right-side view we can see that the book on the furthest right will not be seen from the left side. The answer can only be B.

1 D 2 D 3 E 4 B 5 B 6 C 7 A 8 B   (Page 88)

1 Three thousands less than 41 827 is the same as 41 827 − 3000. It is 38 827.

2 Work through it. You could use a number of solution plans—solving a simpler problem is perhaps best here. Think of the cost as being, say, $3.00 instead of $3030. How could $3.00

be split up so that the boat cost twice the cost of the trailer? Here are the three coins:

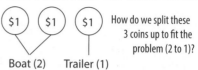

Fairly easy, isn't it? The trailer will cost one of the $1 coins; the boat will cost two. In other words we have divided $3 by 3 and we will have just what was asked for, the boat costing twice as much as the trailer. How do we transfer that simple problem to the one we have been asked? What happened?

We actually split the amount up into three parts—one for the trailer, two for the boat—which is the same as dividing by 3. Try this in your solution. Divide the amount we have in the problem ($3030) by 3 as we did with the $3. This will be $3030 ÷ 3 = $1010. If this is the cost of the trailer, the rest ($3030 − $1010, or 2 × $1010) will be the cost of the boat. Your working gives you a cost of $2020 for the boat, which is double the $1010 which was the cost of the trailer.

Note: You can use this method (called a 'ratio') with all questions where one item is some number times another. In the above problem, the ratio of the boat to the trailer was 2 to 1 (written 2:1). Simply add the parts together (2 plus 1) and divide the total by the parts (the numbers in the ratio). For instance, if the boat had cost 5 times the cost of the trailer, you would add the 5 parts (the boat) to the 1 part (the trailer), making 6 parts; then divide the total ($3030 in this problem) by 6 to give you the cost of the trailer. The cost of the boat would be the cost of the trailer multiplied by 5.

3 Johnny keeps $\frac{1}{4}$ and gives away the rest so he gives away $\frac{3}{4}$. $\frac{3}{4}$ is $\frac{6}{8}$. As his niece and nephews each receive $\frac{1}{8}$, Johnny must have 6 nieces and nephews altogether. He only has one niece so the other 5 must be nephews.

4 As 6 + 4 + 9 = 19, each side must add to 19. The bottom line has 6 so the other two numbers must add to 13. They cannot be

4 and 9 or 6 and 7 as all the numbers have to be different. So they must be 5 and 8 in some order. The two missing numbers on the right side must add to 10. They cannot be 5 + 5 so must be 8 + 2.

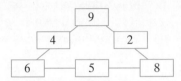

5   The bars were divided equally between 3 of us and I received 206. So the amount that was divided up was 3 × 206 or 618. This was half the bars that were in the chest. So the number in the chest was 2 × 618 or 1236.

6   Work backwards through the problem. There were 75 children on the bus when it arrived at school. At the last stop 10 got on, so there were 75 – 10 or 65 before that. At the second-last stop 15 got on, so there were 65 – 15 or 50 before that. At Mario's stop, Mario and 5 other children got on the bus. So when it arrived at Mario's stop, there must have been 50 – 6 or 44 on the bus.

7   $3 \times 3 \div 3 + 3 - 3$

Multiplying 3 by 3 gives 9, then dividing by 3 gives 3, adding 3 gives 6 and subtracting 3 gives 3, the required answer. Notice that multiplying and dividing are inverse (opposite) operations. One undoes what the other does. Adding and subtracting are also inverse operations.

8   Here the pattern is to subtract the number below the top number from that top number to get the answer at the side. So 23 – X = 12. The question is 'What number can we take away from 23 to get 12?' The answer is 11 so X is 11.

We then need the value of Y but we can't get it straightaway. We will need to find Z first. Following the pattern, 12 – Z = 5 and so Z is 7. We then use the value of Z to find Y. From the pattern, 16 – Y = 7. So Y is 9.

We can now add X and Y: 11 + 9 = 20.

---

1 B 2 E 3 D 4 B 5 C 6 D   Page 90

1   Each hour, train P will travel 75 km and train Q will travel 60 km.

As 75 + 75 = 150, train P will reach Sydney in 2 hours.

As 60 + 60 + 30 = 150, train Q will reach Newcastle in $2\frac{1}{2}$ hours.

So train P will reach Sydney $\frac{1}{2}$ hour before train Q reaches Newcastle.

2   The total distance Sophie jumped is 3 m 45 cm + 3 m 27 cm + 3 m 33 cm. This is 9 m and 105 cm. But 105 cm is 1 m and 5 cm. So the total of all the jumps is 10 m and 5 cm. Now 10 m is 2 m short of 12 m. 5 cm less than that is 1 m 95 cm.

3   This is an area problem. You can use a solution of finding the total number of squares (tiles) in the whole rectangle (floor) and subtracting those still there plus those where the gap is:

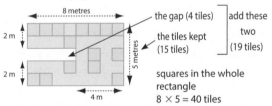

Number of tiles he needs to buy is:

40 – 19 = 21

or simply count the number of spaces.

4   There are 10 marks in the scale of both jugs. Each mark on the smaller jug is 500 ÷ 10 or 50 mL so it has 350 mL of water. As 1 litre is 1000 mL, on the larger jug each mark is 1000 ÷ 10 or 100 mL and it has 600 mL of water. The difference is 600 – 350 or 250 mL.

5   The bar starts at 90 cm. If it goes up 10 cm, it is at 1 m. It then goes up another 10 cm and then 5 cm three times. That is another 25 cm. Kylie jumped 15 cm more than that so she jumped 1 m 40 cm in total.

6   There are 100 cm in a metre. So 1.6 m is 160 cm. The buttons are 8 cm apart. 160 ÷ 8 = 20. There will be 20 gaps between buttons. There will be a

button at the top of every gap and one more button at the bottom of the last gap. There will be 21 buttons altogether.

1 D 2 C 3 A 4 D 5 D 6 B 7 B   (Page 92)

1 The first bus is at Liverpool Street at 11:35 am. 35 + 25 = 60 and 60 minutes is an hour. So it reaches Druitt Street at 12:35 pm. The second bus will arrive half an hour later at 1:05 pm.

2 In a leap year February has 29 days. If 15 February was a Saturday, then counting forward by 7s, so is 22 February and 29 February. 1 March will be a Sunday and so will 8 March. So 7 March will be a Saturday.

3 Cathy left home at half past seven in the morning. Half past seven is 07:30. When she returned home her clock read 17:15. From 07:30 to 17:30 would be 10 hours. Cathy was away from home 15 minutes less than that so she was away for 9 h 45 min.

4 From 5:45 pm until 6:15 pm is half an hour. It will be 6 hours until 12:15 am and another 9 hours to 9:15 am. As 6 + 9 is 15, Cooper will be away from work for $15\frac{1}{2}$ hours.

5 From 9:45 am until 10:00 am is 15 minutes. From 10:00 am until 10:30 am is 30 minutes. As 15 + 30 = 45, Mila took 45 minutes or three-quarters of an hour to walk to her friend's house. If the return journey was 3 times faster, then it would have taken one-third of the time. So it would have taken one-quarter of an hour or 15 minutes. Mila arrived home at 2:15 pm. This means she must have left her friend's house at 2 pm. From 10:30 until 11:00 is 30 minutes. From 11:00 am until 2 pm is 3 hours. Altogether Mila was at her friend's house for 3 hours 30 minutes.

6 There are performances on 3 days each week. If 4 December is a Monday, then so is 11 December and 18 December. 21 December will be a Thursday. There are 2 weeks of performances between Monday 4 and Saturday 16. This means 2 × 3 or 6 performances. In the final week there will be performances on the 18th, 19th, 20th and

21st. So, there are another 4 performances. There will be 10 performances altogether.

7 26 March was a Saturday. The next Saturday, 7 days later, would have been 2 April as there are 31 days in March. Counting forwards by 7, the next few Saturdays were 9, 16, 23 and 30 April. There are 30 days in April so 1 May would have been a Sunday. 8 May would have been the next Sunday and 10 May a Tuesday.

1 D 2 A 3 A   (Page 95)

1 Look at the graph—the column marked with the X has a value between 40 and 50. It must be drama.

2 Consider each statement. One-quarter is 25%. The sales of soup are about 23%, which is nearly one-quarter. So statement X is correct.

The sales of muesli bars are around 14% and the sales of snack packs are 10%. Together they total about 24%. This is less than the sales of cereals, which are about 26%, so statement Y is not correct.

Sales of soups are about 23% and sales of ice blocks are about 16%. Together this is about 39%, which is less than half of all sales. The total of all sales must be 100%. Statement Z is also not correct.

3 Test each value (number) in the age groups against those shown on the graph till you find one that is obviously wrong.

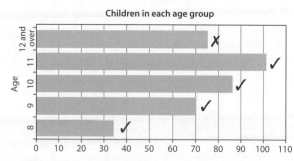

The correct values for 8 years (34), 9 years (70), 10 years (86) and 11 years (101) can be found on the graph. The remaining value, for 12 years and over, shows 75 not 65, so that is the one that is wrong.

YEAR 4 READING **SAMPLE TEST** Page 96

1 A 2 C 3 B 4 D 5 B 6 C 7 A 8 D 9 D
10 B 11 E 12 F 13 D 14 A 15 C 16 B 17 A
18 C 19 A 20 B

1 The mechanical toys consider themselves better than the other toys and treat them as inferiors.
   The other options are incorrect. These options suggest the mechanical toys see the other toys as better than they are, which is the opposite of the truth.

2 Each of the toys mentioned has individual ways of putting on airs. The mechanical toys act in superior ways: the model boat shows off with his use of technical terms and Timothy pretends he is more important than he really is.
   A is incorrect. There is no evidence any of these toys like the Skin Horse.
   B is incorrect. It is the Skin Horse who is old and worn, not these toys.
   D is incorrect. Only the mechanical toys pretend to be real.

3 The Skin Horse understands how you become real because he has experienced this for himself. He knows that when someone loves you over a long period of time then you become real and once you are real, you stay that way. He was made real by the boy's uncle.
   A is incorrect. The Skin Horse doesn't know why you grow old even though he knows that is part of becoming real.
   C is incorrect. Although the Skin Horse knows having things buzz inside you makes toys work, he doesn't understand anything more about how this process works.
   D is incorrect. The Skin Horse doesn't know what you have to do to get repaired.

4 The conversation between the Skin Horse and the Rabbit is about things that are serious and of great importance to them both—almost like matters of life and death.
   A is incorrect. There is nothing playful or enjoyable about their conversation. Rabbit is even left feeling a bit sad and anxious by it.

B is incorrect. Although their conversation could be described as solemn, it is more heartfelt than businesslike.
C is incorrect. Although it is a friendly conversation, it is not lighthearted in any way.

5 The Rabbit is a likeable character mainly because he is modest about himself and his abilities and thoughtful about others, such as when he worries he might have hurt the Skin Horse's feelings.
   A is incorrect. Although the Rabbit believes he is insignificant and commonplace, he is really neither of these things.
   C is incorrect. While he is made of velveteen, this is not the reason he is likeable.
   D is incorrect. Although the Rabbit has friendly impulses towards others, he is shy rather than outgoing.

6 The wind is blowing hard as the poet can feel it rushing past his cheek and causing his hair to blow about wildly.
   A and D are incorrect. The powerful force that is described shows no signs of being teasing or playful.
   C is incorrect. There is no mention of the sound the wind is making in these lines.

7 The poet says he is lost in the dreaming which is making him forgetful of his surroundings and that he is in a potentially dangerous place on the estuary.
   B is incorrect. The poet says he had forgotten about the tide.
   C is incorrect. He is not paying attention to his surroundings so is not listening for the sound of the tide coming in.
   D is incorrect. He is lost in dreams and not paying attention to the water.

8 The tide is characterised as a monster of the deep who emerges 'Snide and snarling' then 'turns' on the poet and pursues him relentlessly, trying to 'grasp' him. His 'Eager tongue curling' adds to this threatening image.
   A is incorrect. The flapping of a scary seagull is different in degree from the nature of the fear and danger the description of the tide inspires.

B is incorrect. While the recollection of the power of the tide's pursuit of him may have dream-like qualities, his experience is too real to be a dream.

C is incorrect. The description of the tide's behaviour and attitude is more menacing than a distant storm.

9   The poet knows he shouldn't have ignored the warning signs that were there for him and recognises how foolish it is to do this in any situation in life.

A is incorrect. Dreams of the future are positive, hopeful things while portents of danger are warning signs that shouldn't be ignored.

B is incorrect. The opposite is implied. To close your mind to what is around you is foolish and can lead to trouble.

C is incorrect. While the poet sees 'portents of danger' as important moments, this is not what the phrase itself means.

10   In the previous sentence the author states that advertising targeting children was slow in coming. This sentence describes one of the earliest attempts to do this that was screened on American television in the 1950s. The next sentence refers to toys available from that time that were to benefit from targetted advertising in the future.

11   In the previous sentence an advertisement is described that showed children playing with a new toy, Mr Potato Head. This sentence describes the features of this toy and what could be done with it. The sentence that follows explains that a few years later toy commercials of this kind were becoming more common and soon became a trend.

12   In the previous sentence the author claims children are conscious of the brand names of things. This sentence points out that this awareness begins at a very early age. The sentence that follows states that, as children grow up, this awareness develops into knowing which brands their peers favour as well.

13   In the previous sentence the author reports there is disagreement as to whether or not advertisements that target children can have

ill effects. This sentence states some people claim they can lead to children making unhealthy choices and even lead to obesity. The sentence that follows describes further problems for children caused by this type of advertisement.

14   In the previous sentence the author says researchers into advertisements for unhealthy foods aimed at children found they used persuasive techniques to which children would be likely to respond. This sentence explains that this has its dangers as children under eight tend to accept advertising as truthful. The sentence that follows reports that as a result of their findings the researchers recommended limits be placed on the kind of advertising screened during children's peak viewing times.

The unused sentence is C.

15   Stick insects look like sticks so they blend into their environment and can be almost impossible to detect.

A is incorrect. Dragonflies are colourful flying insects that don't have good camouflage.

B is incorrect. Planthoppers are very small and fast moving and don't seek out ways to stay hidden.

D is incorrect. Storybook ants are there on the page for all to see!

16   The review of the ant book does not include any reference to scientific research.

A is incorrect. It reports that scientists study dragonflies' flying abilities.

C is incorrect. It mentions research into the way stick insects walk.

D is incorrect. It refers to scientists' research into how planthoppers move.

17   Dragonflies, as measurements of their wingspans over time indicate, have evolved into much smaller insects.

The other options are incorrect. Details of their evolution are not referred to in these texts.

18   Plague numbers of stick insects can damage the environment by, for example, badly damaging eucalypts.

The other options are incorrect. Ways in which these insects can harm their environment are not mentioned.

19 As dragonflies catch their food on the wing it is evident that their flying ability is crucial to their survival.

The other options are incorrect. Planthoppers, stick insects and the storybook ants don't depend on flying for survival purposes.

20 The ants in the story represent human beings. They talk to each other using human voices and they have similar concerns, such as finding ways to survive an expedition or a trial they undertake.

The other options are incorrect. Dragonflies, planthoppers and stick insects described in these texts are, simply, insects.

YEAR 4 THINKING SKILLS SAMPLE TEST   Page 102

1 D 2 C 3 C 4 D 5 B 6 D 7 B 8 C 9 A
10 A 11 B 12 C 13 B 14 C 15 B 16 A 17 A
18 D 19 D 20 C

1 Only D when folded to form a cube will have the same symbol on opposite sides. Practise cutting out and folding nets to understand their properties.

2 According to Lucy's teacher if a student has not participated in at least five school community activities during the year, they do not have a chance of receiving a School Citizenship Award. Therefore none of the students who have participated in less than five school community activities during the year will receive a School Citizenship Award. So this statement must be true.

3 This is quite confusing until you draw a diagram (or a sketch if you prefer):
Bill (B) 2 cm down to Heidi (H), another 4 cm down to Frank (F).

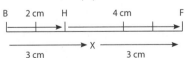

So, Bill is 6 cm taller than Frank and I am exactly between them; in other words 3 cm

shorter than Bill, 3 cm taller than Frank (where the X is) and 1 cm shorter than Heidi.

4 Nina's conclusion is that Jack should run. For this conclusion to work, it must be assumed the tiger is not in a cage. (There is a tiger right behind Jack + the tiger is not in a cage means Jack had better run.)

5 The show is screened for 1 hour for 5 weekdays each week and $1\frac{1}{2}$ hours on Sundays, making a total of $6\frac{1}{2}$ hours per week. This will happen for the weeks beginning Sunday 9, Sunday 16 and Sunday 23. $3 \times 6\frac{1}{2} = 19\frac{1}{2}$ hours (3×6 is 18, 3 halves is $1\frac{1}{2}$). There will be another $1\frac{1}{2}$ hours on Sunday 30, making 21 hours altogether.

6 Consider each of the options to see how many shapes they have in common. Squares P and Q have 2 shapes in common. Squares Q and R have 2 shapes in common. Squares R and S have 2 shapes in common. Squares P and S have 4 shapes in common.

7 This statement provides the best reasons to support the claim that the players should wear mouthguards.

8 The sales assistant has found a book that matches the description from Conor and assumes it **must** be the one he wants. However, it might not be the correct book because there could be other books about dinosaurs with a green cover.

9 Oliver's trip was from 1:30 until 4:00. That is $2\frac{1}{2}$ hours. This was 5 times as long as Ava's trip. $2\frac{1}{2}$ hours is 5 half-hours, so Ava's trip must have taken half an hour. She would have left Windrush half an hour before 4 pm. Ava left Windrush at 3:30 pm.

10 Only Anh's reasoning is correct. We know that Patch always runs in circles when she is excited and she's always excited if she has a new toy. So Anh's reasoning is correct. Ruby's reasoning that Patch must have a new toy is incorrect. There might have been another reason Patch was excited and running in circles.

11 The first crease mark will be in the middle of the paper. When the process is repeated there will be 2 more crease marks so 3 marks altogether. There will be 4 gaps between crease marks. If the process is repeated, there will be crease marks in each of those gaps so another 4 crease marks. Altogether there will be 7 crease marks and 8 gaps around them. If the lines are 3 cm apart, the length of the paper will be 8 × 3 cm or 24 cm.

12 Quickly scanning the ingredients we can see that Nelly only has enough extra ground rice to make half the amount in the recipe. To make 30 biscuits, Nelly would need half of all the ingredients in the recipe. So she would need 225 g of flour, 150 g of icing sugar, 1 tablespoon of ground rice and 175 g of butter. So 90 biscuits would need (450 + 225) g or 675 g of flour. She would need 450 g of icing sugar, 3 tablespoons of ground rice and 625 g of butter. Nelly has enough flour, icing sugar and butter to make at least 90 biscuits. She has just enough ground rice to make 90 biscuits so the greatest number of biscuits she can make is 90.

13 The statement that there has been a 50% decline in butterfly and moth populations provides a reason to support the environmentalist's claim that we need to save butterflies and moths.

14 Garden and watch a movie are both included in the list of things Melia's mum would like to do in the holidays. However, neither Melia nor her dad mentions either one.

15 Find the total for each person other than Isabella.

Name	Test 1	Test 2	Test 3	Total
Isabella	44	42		
Jordan	42	41	46	129
Harper	47	38	42	127
Mary	45	40	43	128
Paige	39	43	48	130

To win the prize, Isabella must have at least 131 marks in total. From the first two tests her total is 44 + 42 = 86. 131 − 86 = 45. So Isabella must score at least 45 marks in test 3.

16 Draw a diagram. Samuel is south-east of Quentin.

17 For the politician's conclusion—that we must try to save the black rhino—to hold, it must be assumed saving black rhinos would be a good thing. (Black rhinos are critically endangered + saving black rhinos would be a good thing means we must try to save them.)

18 We know only students who watch the movie about Australian artists at lunchtime today will have **any chance** of going to the art gallery excursion. So Oliver's reasoning is incorrect. Since he is not going to watch the movie, he will have no chance of going on the excursion. Suma's reasoning is also incorrect. She is going to watch the movie at lunchtime but she has assumed this means she will **definitely** go to the art gallery. However, Ms Brown says this will give her only **a chance** of going.

19 Number the cases from 1 to 5. The gold case is at the far left so it is in position 1. There is one case between the gold case and the red case so the red case must be case 3. The silver case is not next to the red case so the silver case must be in position 5. The blue case is to the right of the red so must be in position 4, leaving position 2 for the green case. There is one case between the red case and the money so the money is in either the gold or silver case. The green case is not next to the money so the money must be in the silver case.

20 Since everyone had to vote for two of the three animals, knowing no student voted for both koala and platypus tells you everyone must have voted for Tasmanian devil. Also, Tasmanian devil must be the animal that everyone voted for because every animal got at least one vote. The outcome will therefore be to adopt a Tasmanian devil.

YEAR 4 MATHEMATICAL REASONING
SAMPLE TEST

Page 107

1 B 2 C 3 B 4 B 5 A 6 D 7 D 8 D 9 A
10 E 11 C 12 C 13 C 14 D 15 A 16 E 17 E
18 A 19 B 20 E

1 Three-quarters of the shape will be 12 squares altogether. She has already shaded three squares so 9 more need to be shaded.

2 In the first half of the year the number of rainy days was 5 in January, 6 in February, 10 in March, 3 in April, 1 in May and 2 in June. That is a total of 27 altogether. In the second half of the year the number of rainy days was 4 in July, 3 in August, 8 in September, 7 in October and 3 in November. So there were 25 rainy days from July to November. It would need to rain on 2 days in December to have the same number as the first half of the year and to rain on 3 days to have more wet days in the second half of the year than the first.

3 7 January is a Friday. Counting forward by 7s, 14, 21 and 28 January are also Fridays. There are 31 days in January so 31 January is a Monday. 1 February is a Tuesday and so is 8 February and 15 February.

4 Counting the squares in the first part of the design, and matching halves, a total of $9\frac{1}{2}$ squares are shaded. When the design is completed there will be 4 lots of $9\frac{1}{2}$ squares. $4 \times 9 = 36$ and 4 halves = 2. Now $36 + 2 = 38$.

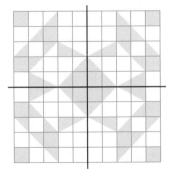

5 There would be two each of these coins: $2, $1, 50c, 20c, 10c and 5c. Add them together

and multiply by 2 or in this case it is easier to double each one then add them. $4 + $2 + $1 + 40c + 20c + 10c = $7.70.

6 Consider each statement: There are more odd numbers than even ones so Selina is more likely to take an odd number than an even one. Statement X is correct. There are 4 numbers less than 5 and 4 numbers greater than 5 so Selina is equally likely to take a number greater than five as a number less than five. Statement Y is correct. There is one card showing 4 and one card showing 9 so Selina is equally likely to take a card showing 4 as a card showing 9. Statement Z is not correct.

7 $37 + 56 = 93$. 93 rounded to the nearest 10 is 90. Harry's answer is 90. 37 rounded to the nearest 10 is 40. 56 rounded to the nearest 10 is 60. $40 + 60$ is 100, so William's answer is 100. The difference between their answers is 10.

8 Find the differences between the numbers. The first difference is 10, the second difference is 9 and the fifth difference is 6. The missing differences must be 8 (third) and 7 (fourth). The missing number is $91 - 8 = 83$ (and check $83 - 7 = 76$).

9 $37 + 26 = 63$. So $82 - \blacklozenge = 63$. This means that $82 - 63 = \blacklozenge$ so $\blacklozenge$ represents 19.

10 From midday until midnight is 12 hours. So it is 12 hours and 10 minutes from when Frances left until midnight. It is another 6 hours until 6 am. 25 minutes to seven is 6:35 am or 35 minutes after 6 am. So altogether Frances's trip took 18 hours and 45 minutes or $18\frac{3}{4}$ hours.

11 Two sides are 2 cm longer so the other two sides must be 2 cm shorter. Or the wire is 4×10 cm or 40 cm long. Two sides are 12 cm long. $40 - 2 \times 12 = 40 - 24 = 16$. So the other two sides add to 16 cm. They must both be 8 cm.

12 500 g for $2 would be 1 kg for $4 and 2 kg for $8 so the larger packet with 2 kg for $7 is the better buy. Susan should buy as many 2-kg packets as she can. The lowest price will be for two 2-kg packets and two 500-g packets. $2 \times $7 + 2 \times $2 = $14 + $4 = 18.

13 Each day Mr Judd travels to a town and home again so the total distance will be twice the sum of the distances to 3 towns. The sum of the distances will be 286 km ÷ 2 or 143 km. The only three distances that add to 143 km are (37 + 49 + 57) km so the towns must be Gallap, Kantor and Riggal.

14 Each number in the sequence is one more than double the previous number. The number after 63 would be 2 × 63 + 1 or 127. To find the number before 63 we need to know 2 × 'what number' + 1 = 63. So 2 × 'what number' is 62, meaning the number is half of 62 or 31. 31 + 127 = 158. So Nate's number was 158.

15 Draw in all the right angles.

E, H and I all have the greatest number of right angles: 4 each. So the greatest number that Molly might have is 3 × 4 or 12.

16 5 + 6 + 7 + 8 + 9 = 35. Each line adds to 22 so the two lines add to 44. One number is counted in both lines. 44 – 35 = 9. As the sum of the two lines is 9 more than the sum of the numbers, the one that is counted twice must be 9. One possible arrangement of the numbers is

17 Practise folding the triangle. The possible fold lines are shown:

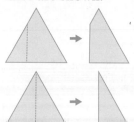

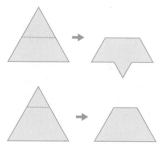

The smaller triangle cannot be formed without some part of the folded paper being seen behind it.

18 In the third column 8 + 4 = 12 so, as 30 – 12 = 18, the middle number of the third column must be 18. One diagonal has 16 and 4 so the middle number must be 10, as 16 + 4 = 20 and 20 + 10 = 30. This means the number in the shaded square must be 2 because, working across the middle row, 2 + 10 + 18 = 30.

16	6	8
2	10	18
12	14	4

19 Ten 50c coins would make $5.00 and 11 makes $5.50. As $9.30 – $5.50 = $3.80, Charlotte has $3.80 made up of 5-, 10- and 20-cent coins. She would need nineteen 20c coins to make $3.80 but she must have at least two 5- and 10-cent coins. So at least 30c is made up of smaller coins, meaning that Charlotte must have at least 2 fewer 20c coins. The greatest number of 20-cent coins Charlotte might have is 17.

20 Daisy can measure 2 litres by filling the 5 litres, emptying it into the 3 litres and 2 litres will remain in the larger bottle. Daisy can measure 1 litre by filling the 3-litre bottle, tipping it into the 5-litre bottle and repeating the process. When the 5-litre bottle is full there will be 1 litre left in the smaller bottle. Daisy can measure 4 litres by first measuring 2 litres (as above and after emptying the 3-litre bottle) and tipping the 2 litres into the 3-litre bottle. She should then fill the 5-litre bottle and use it to fill up the 3-litre bottle. 4 litres will remain in the larger bottle.